Haunted Yet Undaunted

Memoir of a TV Soap Opera Actress

by
Leonie "Lanie" Norton
and
Jim Norton

ISBN: 978-0-578-78450-2

Interior design by booknook.biz

This book is dedicated to
My Mom
Also known as
Babe Hayes and Justine Monro

Who unknowingly believed in me, who paid for my college, a
European college tour, acting school and showed up with groceries for
the "73rd street girls" more often than I can remember!
I love you Mom.

I will see you soon — I hope not too soon —

Given your whereabouts!

This book is also dedicated to Jimmy and Donnie, my devoted brothers
who have always been there for me.

And lastly, my husband Joe, what can I say?
I am the luckiest woman in the world.

Table of Contents

Introduction

by
Bonnie Michaels

Do you want ways to reinvent your life? Do you need survival skills during this time of chaos and change? Is your self-worth in question? Do you want to be entertained and inspired by someone who has done it all? This is the book for you.

During this time of COVID, layoffs, job uncertainty, financial struggles and high anxiety, we need ideas and inspiration for those who have made it through tough times. Leonie Norton has experienced abuse, job loss and uncertainty, financial struggles, divorce, dislocation and disappointment. Not only is Leonie a TV Soap Opera star but she is a superstar at reinventing her life over and over again. Life can be cruel but she faced every difficulty with creativity, courage and entrepreneurship.

This book is more than a memoir of an extraordinary life but a guide to help you face difficulties and setbacks as you navigate a continually shifting world. As your life moves into uncharted territory, read about Leonie's early life going from someone without self worth to a TV soap opera star. You'll laugh and cry as she learns about sex the hard way and navigates the big city life in New York City in the 60s and 70s — with a few disturbing side roads. Find out how she dealt with abuse and disappointment. Laugh as you hear about her reinvented life as a clown and more.

You'll learn that talent is important to be successful but skills, courage to deal with rejections, and a strong self-worth is what counts. She stands up to life, alone, as many of you must do and made it work for her.

Haunted yet Undaunted is an honest, funny, interesting and open-hearted story about Leonie's life journey to happiness and success. You will close the book and realize that you, too, can find your way on this journey of life.

Bonnie Michaels, author of Upside: How to Zig when Life Zags, and A Journey of Work/ Life Renewal, and Solving the Work-life Puzzle.

Chapter 1
The Haunting Begins

I am five years old.

What just happened? "I can't move my arm, Daddy. It's tingling all over!" I hold both my arms close to me. So tight — afraid to move them.

My father is startled. "What did you say?" "I can't move my arm. It's tingling all over."

My father calls my mom! "Lanie can't move her arm. She says it's tingling all over!" Mom rushes in.

"What did you do to her?"

"What you mean? I didn't do anything! Why are you always blaming me?"

"Well, you must've done something if she can't move her arm!"

"For god's sake I didn't do anything!" My father now sounded more angry than frightened. "She was sitting here," pointing to his lap. "All of a sudden she says she can't move her arm and it's tingling all over. What am I supposed to do? What do you want me to say?"

I can't speak. They are arguing. "Oh for heaven's sake!" my mother says. The next thing I know my mom grabs me off my father's lap and rushes me out the door.

"Where the hell are you going?"

My mom was more frightened than angry. "I'm taking her to the hospital. What do you think I'm doing? You stay here with Jimmy and Donnie."

Being careful of my arm, she places me in the back seat of the car. I'm crumpled there, all alone, feeling very small. It was night time. Would you believe I was 5 years old and I can still remember, feel and visualize this whole nightmare?

"I am taking you to the hospital sweetheart." She sounds rushed and scared. "Don't be afraid, everything is going to be all right." She starts the car. "Now, what did your father do to you? What happened for heaven's sake?" She keeps asking me, what did he do? What did *you* do? What did *I* do? I wanted to say. I don't know — I keep telling her, "I don't know! I don't know! I just can't move my arm and it's tingling all over!"

My mother was frightened and upset. I could tell by the way she drove the car. She would push hard on the gas because she was in a hurry. Then

take her foot off the gas when she realized she didn't need a ticket. It was kind of like fast — slow — fast — slow.

Finally, we find ourselves in one of the emergency rooms waiting for a doctor. The doctor walks in. Now it's his turn, "Well, what did *you* do?"

I don't answer. He turns to my mother, "What was she doing?"

I try to answer. "I don't know what I did. I just can't move my arm. It's tingling all over." I just kept saying the same thing over and over to everybody. I had no idea what had happened or was happening. Don't they realize I am only five years old? I didn't know what else to say. All I knew was my arm would not move.

While the doctor and my mother were talking, I found myself trying to remember what had happened. Had I caught my arm on my father's belt buckle while sitting on his lap? I remember I was sitting on his lap facing him. Did my hand brush across his belt buckle? If it did, it didn't hurt or anything. Those were my thoughts at the age of five years when all I knew was — all of a sudden I couldn't move my arm.

The doctor had no answers. He put my arm in a white cloth sling. I spent the next month or so wondering when I was going to be able to use it again. The whole incident was never spoken of again in my house. It remained a mystery — to my parents that is. To me this mystery became a haunting. The paralysis passed, but a bad/guilty feeling remained, that I had done something wrong something bad.

The key to this haunting focused on the fact that, for the life of me, I could not remember my *father's face* — his expression as I sat on his lap facing him! Nevertheless, over the years, as many times as I tried to conjure up that expression, I could not succeed.

This haunting was going to play a significant role in my life on so many levels. Several months later my arm finally regained its feeling as mysteriously as my paralysis appeared, it had left me — I was surprised and thankful. No one wants to go to school with their arm in a sling. I already felt strange and lonely as I was about to enter kindergarten.

Leonie "Lanie" Norton
and Jim Norton

Was I ever to know what happened that unresolved day? Maybe not, but little did I know — "The haunting begins!"

CHAPTER 2
My Father's Voice

"Where was it? Where was my father's voice? I thought there was a special father's voice somewhere inside all men who become fathers. Where was my father's voice? Dad! — I can't hear you. I don't feel you. I don't see you. I can't even touch you. You don't touch me. Are you in there somewhere? Please, answer me!"

That's what I would say to myself at seven years old. I knew what a mother's voice was. I could hear hers. I didn't know what a father's voice was or what he was supposed to do. I understood my mother took care of us, giving us the basics, sometimes making our clothes, taking care of us when we became ill. She would rub my head and give me medicine. Made sure we had dinner and school lunches. But my father — the only thing I felt about him was that he didn't care about me, notice me, or even like me! If this was true, why did I have the feeling that I was supposed to love him and get his love back? Human instinct perhaps!

At the age of 7, I had forgotten all about my paralyzed arm. It wasn't until I was a little older that I would uncover that long buried event. Unknowingly, that episode and those to follow would haunt me the rest of my life.

I didn't understand how the members in a family were to relate to each other. How they were supposed to treat each other. Some kids in school talked about how they did things with their mom and dad. A lot of them had their parents read to them every night. There were no books in my house. Nobody read to us. There were no relationships going on in our family. We did two things together that I can recall. Every Sunday we went for a drive. No, it wasn't any place special. We just drove around town. It was called a "Sunday drive." At the time I had no feelings about it except it was kind of boring. I always sat in the back seat feeling a little carsick. The other thing was eating dinner together. Even that wasn't very pleasant because my brother, Donnie, was such a picky eater. My father was always yelling at him — "eat your peas!" I moved about my childhood life feeling shut off, closed out, unconnected and lonely. I was just sleepwalking my life away when it came to my parents.

I can remember but, "six times," hearing my father's voice as a child. *Six times*! And I thought hard to come up with that many! (Not counting when I paralyzed my arm, 2 years ago.)

The "first time," I remember hearing my father's voice was when my brother and I were fooling around upstairs in our bedroom.

We shared a room together because our house was so small having only three bedrooms for the five of us. Because my one brother, Jimmy, was seven years older and from our mom's first marriage, he got his own room. My brother Donnie and I shared a room because we were only a year and a half apart. I think we had bunk beds.

It was bedtime, Donnie and I had been sent officially upstairs to bed. We weren't really that sleepy. We started throwing pillows at each other, giggling, messing around. We were making a lot of noise after we were supposed to be sleeping. At our house when you were told to go to bed, there were no two ways about it! You went upstairs, brushed your teeth, got into bed — lights out. Really? I was 7 and Donnie was almost 9. Pretty hard to keep two little kids that age quiet. Especially when we were in the same room and weren't even tired!

Donnie, Jimmy and me in our statue-like pose.

We were in the middle of a pillow fight when I heard my father's voice yelling up the stairs from the living room.

"Now you two kids cut that out right now, or I will come up and give you my belt!" Dead silence! Dead — dead silence throughout the house! Well, someone had to answer him. I remember kind of whispering back down the stairs,

"Okay, Dad, sorry, we'll be quiet."

"You better be sorry and you better be quiet that's all I have to say!"

That's when my older brother Jimmy came rushing into our room. He turned on the light. With an angry whisper he said, "What are you guys trying to do get us all in trouble?" He looked at us both with an angry glare.

"We were just fooling around, Jimmy." Then I added, "Sorry." Why was I the one always saying sorry?

"Okay. But cut it out," Jimmy said angrily.

Donnie was trying not to laugh. His laugh was really a nervous reaction from fear that our father would come up and, *deal* with us. Jimmy, still angry, whispered harshly, "And Donnie, stop laughing right now! If he hears you laughing, he's really going to come up here!" Donnie and I shut up. Jimmy shook his head, turning off the light as he left. We never fooled around again.

The connection with both my parents physically and mentally during my early years was virtually nonexistent. I can't even remember my father holding my hand! I would try to get him to play ping-pong with me but his response was always the same —

"Why would I want to play with you? You're no competition!" He'd laugh and look at my brothers for confirmation. I was dismissed feeling worthless!

That was the "second time," I remember hearing his voice. Unfortunately, although I was no competition and worthless at ping-pong, he would seek me out in other ways. Ways I would not understand.

The "third time," I remember hearing my father's voice was at dinner time.

I really only saw my father at dinner time or in our basement playing ping-pong with my brothers. I would just roller skate around to the music on my little pink record player, hoping to be noticed. At dinner time there was no conversation at the table other than, "Finish eating everything on your plate and drink all your milk before you leave the table. You know people are starving all over this world. You should be grateful that you have food on your plate." My father would say that at every single meal. Dinner time was never like the Reagan's — the TV show, *Blue Bloods*! If that show had played when I was a kid, I would have known what I was missing. I could handle dinner time because I would feed half my plate to Lucky, our dog. He was a mutt. Back then practically every dog looked alike. Pretty much no pedigree in those days! Mutt or no mutt, he did have a nose for food! I trained him to sit underneath my chair so I could sneak him food I didn't want to eat. Mushrooms were the worst and of course cauliflower and those small green trees! But Lucky liked any food I gave him, tail wagging. I was his friend for life. Funny, Donnie never knew why Lucky liked me so much. I was not about to tell him. He would have told my father just to get back at me. After all I was his little sister. He was always told to take care of me. "Donnie," my mother would say, "Why don't you let Lanie play with you and your boyfriends?" He hated that. I mean no brother wants his little sister hanging around. Or she would say, "Donnie, remember, whatever you do today, take your sister along with you and your friends!" My mother didn't want me hanging around either! Donnie would drop his head low, lift it up again and whine, "Do I have to?"

"You heard me! And it's do I have to mother!" Having to take your younger sister with you everywhere you go is so embarrassing.

"Yes, *mother*," — spoken with great weariness.

I must say he did get the worst of it at the dinner table. Mom made a lot of peas. Donnie hated peas! My father would get on him to eat all of his food, including his peas. This would go on every night we had peas. I was allowed to leave the table as I had finished everything on my plate, while Donnie was still there staring at his plate of peas and a glass of unfinished milk. I would watch him from the hallway. His head was hanging low and his face was so sad. My poor brother he was always having stomach aches from the stress. I wished I could help him. I just couldn't risk it. After all, our father played with him all the time. He had no complaints. I did not want to share Lucky with him. That just wouldn't work. We might both get caught! I didn't want to ruin it for me. I finally had something that was mine.

Donnie had such terrible stomach aches at dinner my mother finally got wise and started feeding us before our father returned home from work. I didn't realize it at the time, but she must have been looking out for us. Most of the time my father had been drinking before he came home, that was probably why he gave us such a hard time. He thought that's what fathers do. What a laugh. He had no clue about being a father or what they do, nor any apparent desire to seek out how to be one. I think my father actually enjoyed giving us a bad time. He always had this superior look on his face at the dinner table. He had no power over anyone at work, but he could certainly rule over us at home. My stress showed up as mouth sores. They hurt worse than my brother's stomach aches.

I didn't know what a real father was supposed to be in the first place. I guess you can't miss what you don't know you don't have. He just wasn't interested in us unless we could play ping-pong with him, and lose I might add. It was all about *him*. We were never a thought.

A couple of years had passed. I was 9 at the time, as I mentioned, although he didn't want to play ping-pong with me, he would seek me out in other ways.

The "fourth time," I remember hearing my father's voice was one day after school.

I walked upstairs toward my bedroom. My father was in the bathroom, the door was open. I heard him call, "Lanie, why don't you come in and keep me company while I take a shower?" At first, I was pleasantly surprised he was asking me to be with him! That was a first! My delight was stopped short as a weird shiver swept through my entire body! He was asking me to join him while he was taking a shower? Something is wrong about this, something is scary!

He had never asked me to keep him company while he was in the bathroom. Let alone during his shower. So even though I was happy to hear my father's voice wanting my company, I couldn't shake the scary feeling going through me. Should I be afraid? Was something up that I didn't understand?

I entered the bathroom warily. I noticed the shower curtain was closed. I sat down on the closed toilet seat with great apprehension. I noticed the shower curtain move back a little — it moved back a little more. The shower curtain, that had once been totally closed, was slowly being dragged across the curtain rod. I looked up toward the curtain rod. Fingers were moving the curtain. Suddenly the shower curtain stopped opening. Water started falling. My father's stark naked body was partially exposed. There had been no conversation since I entered the bathroom. No, "How was your day?" Or, "How is school going?" There was just an eerie silence. I felt my hands going white clutching both sides of the toilet seat. I could feel perspiration running down my face. My body froze. Then my eyes became aware of a strange rigid piece of flesh protruding from the middle of his naked body. I had no idea what I was seeing! I just knew I could not and should not be there! Totally confused, I panicked, leapt up, and fled the bathroom — turned quickly to my room which was adjacent to the bathroom — I closed my door.

What had just happened? I had no idea! What had I just seen? I had no idea! It is still so vivid in my mind to this day! Why did I panic and run? Why did I have a strange, guilty feeling? My mind suddenly returned to when I was five years old facing my father on his lap — my arm becoming paralyzed, having that same guilty feeling. I sat in my room breathing crazily. My body was shaking all over. I was on the verge of tears! Should I do anything? Should I tell my mother? God no, I will just cause them to argue more. No, no. Never do that! Never tell! How sad we can never tell, and we don't understand why we can never tell! The upshot was, I kept it entirely inside myself.

My mind closed down as I sat on my bed. Utter loneliness blanketed me! I try to remember my father's face. Absent again in my memories. Later that night I was awakened to arguing from downstairs. I heard it most nights as my parents did not get along. This night I thought I would sneak to the head of the stairs and try to hear what they were fighting about. Both voices were fast and loud with lots of anger nothing I could really make out. I went back to my room hoping they were not arguing about me being in the bathroom with my father while he was taking a shower.

I always wondered why I preferred a bath as opposed to showering. The answer popped into my head one day just out of the blue, as I recounted this memory for the first time. I found a lot of things that happened in my childhood, would just pop into my head as my life continued. And I was undaunted in finding out why.

I hated having my door closed because I always felt lonely in the dark, not scared just — lonely. But after most days, I was really tired from school and homework and wanted to sleep. So nighttime fell and loneliness returned. This time as I started to go to sleep, I realized my experiences with my father were either unpleasant or just plain strange. I had never been hugged nor had he ever said he loved me. I wanted him to love me. He seemed to love my brothers. How could I get him to love me? I felt I was nothing to him! Was I really nothing to everybody?

The "fifth time," I remember hearing my father voice was when I returned home from school.

I was walking upstairs toward my bedroom. This time I heard his voice coming from my parents' bedroom. The door was open and he was in bed under the covers. "Lanie, dear, I'm sick today. Why don't you come in and talk to me?" My body froze. I couldn't move. Lanie, dear! — was so creepy!

Nevertheless, maybe this was my chance to be shown some love from my father? Maybe the bathroom incident was some kind of mistake. Or maybe I had overreacted. Maybe I should've stayed. Maybe! Maybe! Maybe! I didn't know. I never told my mom or talked to anyone about it certainly not kids at school.

Now, all he was asking was for me to come in and talk with him. I could do that. What could be wrong with that? Why am I always afraid of him when I really want to be with him? Confusion ran through my mind.

I edged toward the open door. I entered quietly, slowly moving toward the bed, when he suddenly started patting the bed covers and said, "Why don't you lie down on the bed with me so we can talk?" I froze in my footsteps! I could not respond.

There was that look again on his face that I don't want to remember. I slowly moved toward the foot of the bed to get away from him. I continued to circle around the bed getting farther away from him. I froze once again!

"Aw, come on now," he said, "sit down over here!" Frustration was building in his voice. He started to pat the *other* side of the bed close to where I was standing.

"I don't feel well. You are my little girl, aren't you?" He never said that to me before. — His little girl? Where did that come from? What's going on? After all the time I had wanted to be a boy, now he calls me his little girl.

"Why don't you lie down with me?" Now there was a bit of anger in his voice. He patted the covers harder and faster on the side of the bed where I was standing. I didn't want to look at his face. It made me feel really uncomfortable. The bathroom incident flashed across my mind. This time he was in his pajamas. Did other daughters lie down with their fathers? I couldn't dispel the feeling that something wasn't right. It was the sound of his voice. Nothing seemed to fit. At these weird times his voice had a tone that made me feel I would be doing something bad. I felt somehow I was being asked to do something I would feel guilty about later. Climb on the bed with him? I simply couldn't do it. I simply could not lie down on the bed with my father! Would under the covers be next? At the same time, I was nagged by the feeling that once again I was going to disappoint him. I was so ambivalent. Part of me wanted to lie down on the bed with him — the part that wanted to be loved. Another part of me, the part that felt I would be doing something wrong would not let me do it! I had to voice my feelings. I couldn't stand there any longer.

"No, I am sorry. I can't. I have to go to my room and study." I left quickly. As I closed my bedroom door, I could hear him calling,

"Aw, come on! What's the matter with my little girl?"

I covered my ears! I didn't want to his voice *or* see his face. His face always looked so strange during these mysterious requests. I never knew what he was thinking when he asked me things like this. Things that always made my stomach twist. And the way he said things brought about a weird, guilty feeling. I felt guilty, but don't know what for. It was all so crazy!

That evening I could hear them arguing again. I knew it had to be about me. That next morning I was to get the biggest and worst shock of my life! It was Saturday morning. I had slept in. I was excited about having pancakes for breakfast which was one of my special treats on the weekend. I started to rush downstairs. My father caught my eye as I passed their bedroom. I stopped dead in my tracks. What? My father was packing his suitcase! Were we going on a trip I hadn't been told about? What was he doing? I didn't know what to think or do! I just waited for him to finish. I stood there confused, anxious. I was so afraid that *I* had done something that was causing him to pack a suitcase. Was he leaving us? I am always doing something wrong. He closed his suitcase. Lifted his coat and hat and suitcase from the bed, turned, and spoke to me — this was to be the last time I was to hear my father's voice, for many years.

"Your mother and I have not been getting along. So it's best that I leave."

And down the stairs he went. I couldn't believe what I had heard. I slowly took one then two steps and watched him go down the stairs and vanish out the front door. The whole time I said nothing. Why didn't I say something? My father was leaving us! I didn't see my mother anywhere. Isn't she going to stop him? Isn't anyone going to stop him? She had said nothing to me about his leaving. I just stood there seemingly forever! What was this? He just walks out! I was devastated. No chance now ever to win his love! I will never get his love! And it will be all my fault! All my fault, was to ring in my ears for a very, very long time. Our family was broken! And, of course, it was my fault. My brother would never say it, but I knew he felt it was all my fault.

My father's leaving was so out of nowhere I couldn't get my head around it. Leaving — no notice — walking out the door? Is he coming ever back? Will we ever see him again? Or if we don't see him, is he going to call us? What about my birthday and Christmas and…? What does *leaving us* even mean?

I rushed back upstairs to Donnie's room which was right next to the staircase. We each had our own room now as Jimmy had gone off to college. Donnie's door was already open. He was sitting on the end of his bed all quiet, legs hanging down looking at the floor. I stared at him. "Did you know dad was leaving?"

"Yes."

"Why is he leaving?"

"I don't know." My brother wouldn't look at me. He sat on the edge of his bed. I was confused. Our father was leaving the family, but my brother was displaying no outward reaction. He wasn't crying. He didn't seem angry. He didn't look at me and say something comforting or anything at all. No communication again between us. We did horse around once in a while, but mostly I was just a pain in the neck younger sister. I felt like I might cry. I didn't want Donnie to see me cry. I stood a little longer hoping he might look at me. Then I swallowed hard, turned and left the room.

What had I done? Why was our father leaving? Where was he going? Questions just filled my mind with no answers. Mom had never said a word about it.

Then the truth dawned on me. My father's not leaving because they can't get along — my father's leaving because of me! I made him leave! Of course! I made him leave! Oh, my poor mother! I had ruined her life! He is leaving her because of *me*. What in the world had I done? Still not knowing what I really had done to make my father leave us, I kept returning to the same conclusion that it had to be *my fault!*

As an adult, a person who had been emotionally and sexually abused as a child, I often ask myself, why did I not tell and get help from anyone? Why didn't I ask my mother why my father left us? I never even spoke to her about it. Why didn't I tell her the things he would ask me to do with him? As a family we never spoke our minds or asked questions.

When it comes to children and the family, think back as hard as you can. Think about all you didn't know. Think about all you wanted to know. Think about how you wanted to be treated. And start with love! Parenting is the balancing act on a tightrope — missteps can cause a lot of damage to you and anyone you fall on. Next to marriage, parenting is the hardest job there is! I have to say let love lead the way, remembering that part of love is teaching your kids to love themselves and respect others. You need to set boundaries for them so they become the kind of human being they would like to love.

Chapter 3

A Passionate and Desperate Wish

My father's leaving was never spoken of. No reason was ever given or told to us by our mother. And my brother and I were both afraid to talk to my mother. It was as if he had disappeared — zap! Just like that! And we were supposed to go on with our lives as if nothing had ever happened. Just like when I paralyzed my arm. Another mystery, another silence, and no conversation.

Each day that went by thoughts about my father's leaving cluttered my mind. I had trouble concentrating in school. I found myself by myself in my room trying to understand what had happened. Was it really me — was it really my fault? Could it be that he was angry that I didn't join him under the covers? Did he think I didn't love him? Should I have stayed and talked to him in the shower? Maybe just turn my head instead of fleeing from the bathroom? Maybe I asked him too many times that I wanted to play with him. Maybe I was just too annoying. Maybe I was just nothing! Maybe, maybe — maybe!

Other days I found myself asking what can I do to fix this? Somehow I felt it was my responsibility to get him to come back. I would comply with his requests. I decided there was nothing wrong in what he was asking. I would become "his little girl." If he came back, there would be no more arguing, just smiles all around and my father paying more attention to me. Then I was suddenly struck by a magic wand! I knew exactly what I had to do — I had to become a boy! That's it! I will become a boy! Why didn't I think of that before he left? Silly me! Maybe it wasn't too late. I was about 10 years old at the time. That's what my father likes boys — so that's what I'll become. *A boy*!

I had made my decision. Going about becoming a boy was none too easy. How was I going to pull this one off? Become a boy? I began to think what makes a boy better than a girl? Boys are stronger, more important, more looked up to. They are allowed to do daring things. Daring and dangerous things! That's it! I thought if I did a really dangerous thing, I would change into a boy. Just like that!

Believe this or not, I still can't believe it myself — I was so certain if I did a very daring and dangerous thing that I would *physically* change into a boy. I was totally and completely convinced I would *actually* turn into a boy. No questions asked. It would happen. I was doing that to be loved, and accepted. Can you imagine throwing yourself away and become someone else? Just to be loved. Wait a minute, we do that all the time! But, turning into a boy, well that's a first. I was just a kid remember, with a very vivid imagination and a very desperate need to be loved by my father. I write about it — I talk about it but just how desperate I must have been to think I would change into a boy.

It was the foolproof answer. I would abandon my girl-self so I could be loved by my father. Without hesitation I would change who I was. The sad part — I really didn't know who I was. And I was getting no help from my parents.

Okay, so I was going to do a daring thing and change physically. I didn't even consider changing, mentally — into a boy. And in my thinking, my problems would all be solved. I would be loved and respected by my Father. Why I might even beat him at ping-pong! Now wait a minute.

I don't want to make him mad. If I beat him at ping-pong, he may not want to play with me anymore. So I will just let him win all the time. He'll really love me for that. He never liked it when my older brother Jimmy beat him. He was a real sore loser.

Remembering the one thing I was *never* allowed to do was the one thing I *would* do. It was dangerous, I knew that much. I was never allowed to cross the big highway called Route 17 on my bike. My mom would talk about killing myself. That's what would happen if I crossed Route 17 — a four lane highway — on my bike. I would be hit by so many cars that they wouldn't even recognize me after it was over. So that's what I'll do. That's daring enough for me! Why I had seen boys on bikes ride right across the highway into oncoming traffic going fast as they could and make it right across in a flash!

I waited for the next Saturday. Fortunately, it wasn't too far off. Three days to wait — three long, long, days! I was bursting to share my amazing plan with somebody, but I had no friend at school who I felt close to or that I felt I could trust. Besides, the surprise would be better if they didn't know what I was going to do. Of course, the three days were filled with all sorts of events and incidents that in no way would help me change into a boy. So going across Route 17 by myself on my bike, became my only option.

When Saturday rolled around I was ready. My bike was ready, all tuned up and ready for the long ride to Route 17. It was about a 40 minute bike ride. I had no problem with that. I would pass all my favorite places to play and visit. There would be Pat's Deli and the favorite ice cream place called Terwilliger and Wakefield. The Duck Pond we ice-skated on in the winter was just across the way so it was going to be a great ride. I did it all the time with my friends, Ellen and Carolyn. But I had never gone over the hill to the big shopping center along the highway. No, I surely never had done that. But today — right now — my life was going to change radically — I was going to become a boy! I was going to be loved!

As I started out the door, my mom asked me where I was going. "A bike ride."

"Okay," she said. "Just be careful. A lot of crazy drivers out there!"

"No problem, Mom. I'll be careful!"

I got on my bike and started peddling. As I got closer and closer to Route 17, my crazy plan to become a boy tightened my stomach into a huge painful knot. Don't pay any attention to it, Lanie. You're too close. You can't quit now. I pedaled harder and faster. I reached Ridgewood Avenue, made a right turn and straight down to Route 17. I passed a few friends, Kathie, Carolyn and Alison. We waved. A smile broke across my face! I bet they are wondering where I am going. The next time Alison sees me, the shock will probably knock her braces right off her teeth! Come to think of it my girl friends think my brother Donnie is so cute. Boy are they going to be surprised when they see me again! They'll all want to be *my* girlfriend! I won't be me — a 10-year-old girl — I will be the new me, a 10-year-old boy! A brief uncomfortable feeling shot through my body. What am I doing? Am I really going to do this craziness? Well, too late to think about that now. It's magic, remember! I have a plan, and I'm going to go through with my plan. I had to be brave. Boys are brave! Concentrate! Pedal faster! I pedaled as fast as I could to reach the highway. It's got to work it just has to!

The highway! The scariest place to cross with a bicycle I had ever seen! Four lanes of heavy, terrifying traffic — two going to the left of me and two going to the right of me. Four lanes of cars and trucks, huge long trucks! I was going to have to cross to get to the other side — alive! To me the cars seemed like they were going hundreds of miles an hour! I watched as they swerved in and out of lanes, giving each other the horn. Zooming cars and huge 18 wheelers — swirling paper and debris all around me! The whole scene made me nauseous. The wind from the speeding vehicles pulled at my face. Unreal and terrifying, yet weirdly exciting — raucous noise, racing vehicles — no traffic lights to slow things down! Of course, I didn't know about, no traffic lights on an interstate highway like this. If you were going to cross it, you had to cross it right through the oncoming traffic with no traffic lights to give you a break.

Two lanes on one side, two lanes on the other, I had to cross four lanes of cars no hesitation allowed! Now that is certainly a magic trick that should turn me into a boy! Certainly enough magic to bring about my passionate wish! And I — me, the 10-year-old girl was about to become *the magician*! I was about to pull a 10-year-old boy out of my "magic hat" at the other side of the highway!

I still find it unbelievable, that I truly thought this magic was going to happen! When my mind relives that moment over and over again, I could just cry. I am not her anymore. But I see this little girl, like in a movie, waiting to cross the forbidding highway, waiting to possibly kill herself, with the desperate need to be loved by her father. The reality of the situation is staggering and unimaginable!

Deep breath now — lots of deep breaths. Wait! Wait for the right time to blaze forward into that impossible journey! Remember you only have one chance! Okay, time to get serious. Now go! — No, wait! — Now,—?

I kept searching for any kind of opening that would allow me to speed across *four* lanes of 65 miles per hour or more, traffic! No, not yet pausing,… this one? No, no, not yet — too many cars. Wait! — Looking again — maybe now? No, not yet. Keep looking! Keep looking —

NOW!

Finally, there appeared to be an opening that if I really went fast, I could make it across *all four* lanes. Yes, this is it! — GO! I jumped on my bike and started across the highway. Ride like you've never ridden before, Lanie! Ride like the wind as they say! Ride! Ride! RIDE! I gave it all I had, looking straight ahead. Faster —faster — faster! I'm close. Almost there! Almost there! Closer- Faster! Keep pedaling! Only TWO more lanes to go! Don't look just ——— GO!

Heavy breathing was causing a stitch in my side. Two more lanes Lanie, two more lanes and you're home free! Or better yet, home free and you will be a BOY! Yes, now one more lane! Don't think — just peddle — peddle — YES!

The stitch in my side became crippling. I stopped hard, my legs hit the ground — I threw my bike down. My body fell forward and there I was.

I had done it! I had really done it!

As I lay on the ground waiting for my breathing to slow down, I closed my eyes. I can still feel and see myself lying there on the grass. I lay there waiting for something to happen. Did I feel any different? Did I look any different? I tried to breathe normally, but every time I took a breath, the stitch in my side hurt. Calming myself down as best I could, I realized it was time to open my eyes and — and what? See if I was a boy? Yes! See if I was a boy! I didn't really feel any different. Hyperventilating and shaking all over — was I a boy? I focused on giving myself the courage to open my eyes. I felt sick to my stomach, and very alone.

Finally, I opened my eyes. I stared straight up toward the sky — afraid to look down or left or right or at any part of my body. I lifted one of my arms and looked at it to see if it had changed into the arm of a boy, nothing, then I lifted a leg — and then I burst into tears! I wasn't a boy. No way did I feel like a boy. No magic surrounded me I was still a girl —I lay there in silence, crying. Disappointment was all I could feel. My breathing had quieted, reality was starting to return. I had failed. Where do I go from here?

I was so sure that I would turn into a boy. There was no magic in my crossing the four lanes of impossibly heavy traffic — I was still a girl! Risking my life hadn't worked. I hadn't done it! I realized I was still a girl. I cried out my disappointment, only to realize that now I had to get back to the other side of the highway — alive! You are going to have to do this all over again and there's going to be nothing on the other side but a 10-year-old girl, named Lanie Norton!

All I could think about is that I was so desperate to be loved by my father, and this was my only solution to achieve that love. I allowed myself to replace what 10-year-old intelligence I had with my desperate emotional need to be loved by him. There was no magic to be found in crossing the busiest highway in the world, four lanes of traffic on my bicycle. What was I thinking? The only magic left now is — surviving!

I just can't believe it! I kept shaking my head from one side to another in frustration. I have to cross back *again* to the other side! *I could still get killed!* Now I was really frightened! Before I had a reason to cross, at least I thought I did. Now all I have is the second fright of my life making it to the other side.

I remember that scene so vividly. There I was holding the handle bars of my bicycle, terrified and bewildered at the whole prospect of having to risk my life all over again for no reason and so lonely and disheartened. It brings tears to my eyes as I relive that moment. How desperate I must have been to put myself through that ridiculously dangerous unnecessary event. To think I was not good enough to be loved. I and only I, give my father that enormous power over me.

So there I was now having to cross the big bad highway — still as a girl. Nothing at stake but to stay alive! These days I probably would have called my mother on my cell phone but those days…? I stood there, breathing dirt and carbon dioxide, laughing at what a ridiculous situation I was in — the laugh was really whistling in the dark so I wouldn't start crying again. Once again I bolstered my courage. I told myself, if I did it once I can do it again. This time I wasn't as terrified. At least I knew it was possible if I paid attention. For some reason, it was easier this time. I may not have turned into a boy, but I certainly felt braver and proud of myself for staying alive.

So there I was pedaling home. The truth is I was more afraid of my mother finding out what I had done. I did tell Donnie. I had to because I was so proud of myself. He told me I was crazy and spilled the story to my mother of course. When my mother heard it she dropped everything, and all hell broke loose! I had never heard her yell so loud and look so angry and scared.

"What on earth made you do that?" She was near tears. "What if you had been killed?"

I didn't see the tears behind her anger. She made me feel ridiculous and stupid. Where was my hug? I am still alive! Why didn't she hold me? What if I had been killed? Donnie said nothing. He just stood there. There was no discussion after that, and no one asked me why. Nobody wanted me there I may as well have been invisible.

I decided to run away. I buttered some saltines crackers — I loved buttered saltines — packed them up with a drink, and off I went. This was really the only answer since no one really wanted me around, especially now that I hadn't turned into a boy. I told my brother I was running away, and he said, "Good idea!" and laughed. You see? He really didn't care about me either. I was his little sister always in his way. Thank goodness we all grow up. My brother Donnie and I have a great deal of love for each other now. In times of stress and need, he has always been there for me and still is to this day.

I will confess, I was glad they never asked me why I had crossed Route 17 at rush hour. So out the door and down the front steps I went. I guess I got about a third of the way down the street when I heard my mother yelling for me. Apparently, my brother didn't want me to leave after all and had told my mother.

"Oh, no you're not Lanie! You get back here right this minute! You hear me? Get yourself home right now before, before! I don't know what I will do but you better get home this instant. Do you hear me?" I can still hear her yelling from our porch and she could yell!

Partly thankful that my mother was yelling at me to come home, I turned around and came back as fast as I could. I guess she really did want me around after all. The day had been stressfully long, and I don't think I really wanted to leave home anyway.

Chapter 4

After My Father Left

Fortunately, after my father left us, the haunting was temporarily suspended because I didn't have to see or hear from him for many years. Besides that, as guilty as I felt about the divorce, my mom made it possible for me to breathe easier by never mentioning him and keeping him out of my life and thoughts.

As I write my story and relive these memories, I understand I will never know if my mom knew what was going on between my father and me. Was all that arguing about me? Did she quietly save me from further encounters with him? I only knew he was gone.

I never missed him. After all I really never saw him. And when I did it was never pleasant. At least now I was safe. I didn't have to wonder what he was going to do next. What ploy would he come up with to get me to watch him or be with him in some inappropriate situation? No, I never missed him because I never had any kind of a relationship with him in the first place. He was gone. I simply gave up trying to win his love. This unfortunately would play a big part in my adult life with the men I would meet.

In those days divorce was a stigma. You were said to be from a *broken home*. That was not a good thing. And this was my mother's second divorce. My older brother Jimmy was from her first marriage. He was about five years older than my brother Donnie and seven years older than me. Thinking about that now, my mom must have been a really brave woman. She stood up for herself not wanting a marriage without love twice, not tolerating male dominance with the understanding that she would become a single mother raising three children. Women in those days were tolerating life in empty, loveless relationships. She didn't have time for stigmas. She had her own pressing problems — keeping a roof over our three little heads!

So there I was coming from a broken family. I, of course, was the one who *broke* it. The fear of going back to school loomed before me. I had a best friend Ellen that I would ride bikes to school with. Was she still going to want to ride with me? Would she still play with me? I was about to find out. I went to her house before school started. I asked her if her mother would still let her play with me and ride to school together. She said sure why wouldn't she? I told her my parents are getting a divorce. She answered, "Oh, well I guess I'll have to ask her." I don't think my friend even knew what the word meant or really what I was asking. I just remember that a woman from a divorce was *not a nice person*. It meant she slept around. I didn't know what that meant at the time. Of course there was no shame on the husband. Men can do no wrong. Wow, it never ends does it? No wonder we of the female gender have been struggling so hard for so long and continue to do so.

Ellen returned with a yes. A smile appeared on my face. Well, that's a start, I thought.

The divorce hit me the hardest one day when I was sitting in a school assembly in 6th grade. I don't to this day know what triggered my bursting out in tears and walking quickly up the aisle the 4th row from the front. That was a painfully long walk. Why couldn't I have been sitting in the last row? Keeping my head down as I walked out of the room, I was hoping no one would notice.

Or did I want people to notice? I think I did. I wanted them to feel sorry for me and like me. Where do I go now? And will any of the teachers follow me to see what is wrong? I ended up in the principal's office. I thought that was the best place to be. Someone would certainly find me and see what was wrong. What was wrong? That's what I wanted to know. I just started crying because my family was breaking up and I was responsible.

As I entered the room there was no one there. They were all at the assembly. I found myself walking close to the window. Should I just jump out and end it all? No one would miss me and all my pain would stop. As the thought grew inside me, someone entered the room. It was the lady principal. I turned to her and started crying again. I just wanted to kill myself.

"What is the problem? What's wrong?"

There was a long pause. I just couldn't answer.

"Lanie, what happened?" She asked.

I told her my parents were getting a divorce and it was my fault.

"Oh, sweetheart!" she said.

Teachers always call kids sweetheart or honey and it was really nice to hear that from a lady teacher. She told me she was sure that was not the case. I was not responsible for the divorce. She went on to explain how sometimes in marriage grownups have problems they feel they can't work out and have to get divorced, but it is *never* the fault of the children. I really needed to believe her because I really didn't want to kill myself. That bicycle event was bad enough, and now I wanted to jump out the principal's window! She helped me dry my eyes and told me to go back to the assembly. She suggested that I sit in the back so as not to draw attention to myself and interrupt the program.

Of course, after the program ended everyone wanted to know what had happened to me and was I all right. That felt really good. Maybe I was on my way to being happy. As I walked out of school that day, I looked over to my left and noticed the principal was watching me from her office window. I also noticed that her office was on the *first* floor. Yes, you heard me, the first floor! Good thing I didn't jump! Not much suicide going out of there! I had to laugh at myself. I would have looked pretty stupid to the kids at school. It was simply another stupid idea to try to fix everything. And simply another dramatization of my feelings that needed to be heard. Yes drama. My mother always said I was a *drama queen*! I just wanted someone to notice me and love me. Was that too much to ask for at 10 years old?

CHAPTER 5
An Actress Is Born

Out of those dramatic and traumatic episodes of wanting to be a boy and wanting to kill myself! — *An Actress Is Born!*

Drama queen! That's what my mother called me. If that's what I am as a female in this crazy world, why not become a real actress! It made perfect sense! Performing in front of people was going to be my way of acting out my emotional needs. Letting all those feelings carve out a career.

I had no doubts of my eventual success as an actress! At the age of 10 I was pedaling home from school, all the while planning my first performance. My first stage event was to be presented on the side porch of our house in Ridgewood, New Jersey. Finally, I was feeling okay not being a boy and willing to go forward as an actress. I was looking forward to my plan of reaching the big-time on stage!

My acting career started on my screened-in porch at the side of my house with two windows looking into the living room. These windows gave me the ability to have action coming from the windows as well as on the porch. I wrote, directed, produced and, of course, starred in my own production. I did have to give small parts to my girlfriends down the street. After all, someone would have to introduce me and be in my chorus. They were thrilled. Some dressed as cowgirls, others put on their prettiest dress.

I sang and danced and paraded myself all over the side porch. Waving my arms and showing myself in and out of the windows. My first production starring me was one of the best times of my life! Show tickets were a nickel! And the entire show lasted 15 minutes! Neighbors came, parents came, and siblings came too. We bowed deeply at the end of the show to a standing ovation (not that we had a prejudiced audience or anything!). How I loved my mother! She had called the Ridgewood Herald (our local paper) and got our picture in it. (You can see it in the collage below, *Little Theatre Group with a Purpose*.) We gave all the money to a local charity. It was a total of 75 cents. To have your picture in the paper was a really big deal when you were young. At that moment I was the most important person in the whole world. I mean seriously, I was the whole world! When you are young, you are the whole world, and you are pretty much always the center of that world.

My plan to be a star on Broadway continued in high school. Ridgewood, New Jersey is really close from downtown New York City. So Broadway seemed like it was right across the George Washington Bridge from me. My school years were to afford me many opportunities to perform. I wanted people to like me and think I was someone special. I was in the school talent shows, plays, and the drama club. (See pictures below.) I firmly believed that male roles were more important and had more meaning than female roles. So what did I do in my ninth grade talent show? Instead of performing the female lead from *The Merchant of Venice*, I took the male protagonist role, Shylock, and did his famous speech. The male speech was so much more poignant and powerful than that of the female protagonists. I dressed like a man and spoke "… If it will feed nothing else, it will feed my revenge. He hath disgraced me and hindered me half a million… And what's his reason? I am a Jew."

Oh, I can still see and feel myself on stage, reveling in every syllable. I was really in my glory! My friends and other people in the audience came up to me and told me how great I was. Apparently, I was so high on myself that the timbre of my voice changed when I responded to their comments. I became aware of this because my mother, after my *fans* left, said, "What happened to your voice? You don't sound like yourself." I of course said,

"I don't know what you are talking about!"

"Well I never heard you sound like that before."

Well…maybe I lowered my voice a little. Maybe I put on an English accent to make myself sound more professional. I remember it so well. But, ah yes, even then, I knew how to show off.

During my sophomore year in high school I attended The American Academy of Dramatic Arts in New York City. It was so wonderful to study all the things I loved to do. I have to thank my mom for that. Unfortunately, she wasn't exactly a real pushy backstage mother.

One evening the phone rang and my mother answered, "Hello." Then I watched her listen for a few moments. I heard her talk about my school in New York. She said, "I don't think that's a good idea. I am sorry. No," and hung up.

"Mom who was on the telephone?"

"Oh, your drama teacher at that acting school you go to. He asked me if you could be in a Broadway show."

"And you said —?"

"You heard me. I said, no. You're fifteen, Lanie. You can't be going into New York City by yourself at night. Are you crazy?"

I was dumbfounded. I stared at her in painful disbelief. I finally found my voice well, really just a whisper, "What was the show?"

My mother didn't answer. She continued doing the dishes or whatever. Later I found out from my drama teacher that the show was *Bye-Bye Birdie*. I would have been one of the girls swooning over Conrad Birdie. I was devastated! I could've been on Broadway at 15 years old! Are you kidding me! And my mother wouldn't allow me to go!

"But Mom……"

"Lanie, not another word out of you, now help me with these dishes. You must realize that it simply isn't possible that you, a beautiful young girl, child really, go into New York City by yourself in the middle of the night, by the way, — and have to return home also in the middle of the night. You hear the news you know what happens in New York City to young girls who are by themselves, riding on buses, riding in subways, walking down the street." I really didn't. "I'm really sorry, but I'm your mother, and if anything happened to you, I would never be able to forgive myself."

I clammed up and moped about the house for quite a while. My mom and I never spoke about it again, as usual, no communication. I lost a chance to sing and dance on Broadway for heaven's sake, *Broadway!* I watched this extraordinary opportunity taunt me as it flew out the window! At the time, neither my mother nor I understood to what extent that phone call portended for my future. What fabulous acting path this early signal of my talent recognition would lead me down. So my chance to be on Broadway in *Bye-Bye Birdie* went bye-bye. Nevertheless, always undaunted, my dreams were bubbling over on the front burner! Somehow I knew to the very core of my being that this phone call gave me a promising glimpse into my future as an actress. Furthermore, I realized I would need to take the bus on my own the next time I needed to get to any out-of-state theater. There was no way I would miss out on my next opportunity to be on stage — whether Broadway or anywhere else.

New York City gleamed like the Emerald City in *The Wizard of Oz.* Every time my school had a field trip to the city, I would always lose my breath coming down the hill on Route 3 as the New York City skyline came into view. It was filled with tall buildings spanning from one side of your vision to the other. I always felt a tingling as if someday that city would be mine. The city worked its magic on me every time I entered. My heart always raced, knowing that my next chance to ride the wind was right around the corner. And the haunting memories of my father were not going to stop me.

The next page has a few photos of my early performances in talent shows and plays at school. I also played piano for the school musicals. My favorite is, Little Theatre Group with a Purpose, the news paper clipping. I believe the smaller picture was from a performance of, *Tea House of the August Moon.*

Chapter 6
My Early New York City Life

That *moment* came when I would attend Centenary Junior College for women. Every middle class family in 1960 knew that immediately after high school "every graduating senior *must* go to college." My grades weren't all that great so I was only able to get into a junior college. My heart wasn't into going to college in the first place. Everything about life for me was becoming an actress so my Junior College classes were mostly spent in drama and chorus.

I was really excited when our school chorus was going to tour Europe for five weeks singing at various events in countries that the school had booked. Lucky for me, I was picked to be in a trio as well as the chorus when we toured. Thank goodness my mom came through with the money to go! As children we know little about money or what our parents have to do to get it. Thanks Mom for having as many as three jobs at a time! All I could think about was that I had enough money to go on the tour. What a fabulous time that was! Touring Europe was certainly not something I ever imagined I would be doing. That was only for rich people.

Serendipitously, my college roommate, Susan Hallaran, was an actress on a soap opera. Of course, I was totally bug-eyed and swept away listening to and treasuring her every word. When we got back to school, she took me on set with her. Her friendship reinforced my belief that I was going to become an actress.

Her cute boyfriend came to the college for a dance one weekend. Centenary was a girls' school. So for dates we had to ask the boys from the surrounding boys' schools. The night before the dance the girls got together in one of the dorm rooms and started talking about boys. All of a sudden the word *penis* came into the conversation. I don't even remember what they were saying, but they were laughing. I felt my blood rise to my face. Somehow I was scared. I got up quickly and left the room. Later my roommate asked me why I had left. I said I had homework due and had forgotten to finish it.

At the dance that week end, all the couples were dancing really crazy and moving all different ways that I had never seen. At that time Elvis Presley was really popular. All of his below the waist moves were being imitated. I just stood there feeling strange as my roommate's boyfriend moved in a sexual manner. I didn't realize that his movements were sexual. I felt embarrassed and uncomfortable. He had a look on his face that reminded me of my father. As he danced in front of me, he could tell I felt very self-conscious watching him. He seemed to enjoy watching me be self-conscious and embarrassed. My roommate looked puzzled by my behavior — why wasn't I dancing? I had no idea about being in or moving in a sexual way. From then on I opted out of dating and dancing, preferring to help the girls with their hairdos, making money for reaching my dream and never thought about it again. I missed out on watching Elvis Presley because I just felt strange when I saw him perform, so I never watched him again. Thinking back to that — to those moments, I was probably aroused and had sexual feelings. Feelings within me that I could not understand, nor did I want too. I know that is a little hard to believe, who wouldn't want to be aroused by Elvis. I didn't even realize I was being aroused. I wasn't taught anything. Nada!

Marsha, a high school friend, and I dated some cadets at the West Point Military Academy in our senior year. I had no idea what my date expected of me. I always loved kissing, but when that was not enough, I would break up with the guy. My sexual understanding and participation was sorely lacking. Somehow that information had never gotten around to me and I was already 18. I was never told what happens after kissing and I was afraid to find out.

The school play was holding auditions and hallelujah. I got the lead in the musical *The Boy Friend*. Since we had no boys at school we bussed in boys from a new drama school that had just opened in New York City. It was called The American Musical and Dramatic Theater Academy. During and after rehearsals my male lead told me all about what he studied in his acting school. Everything he told me sounded exactly what I was looking for. We became friends and he got me an audition. My mom came through again, God bless her constant support in that area. I asked her if I get accepted, could I pay for my living expenses and she pay the tuition! I had no idea how much it cost, but she said yes. She didn't really understand my acting desire but she always rose to the occasion. Maybe she was trying to make up for the *Bye Bye Birdie* fiasco.

My mother never worried about my career because I could always marry Steve the pharmacist in town, and become a secretary. Yes there would always be Steve the pharmacist with bright red hair and 6ft 2in. tall. He always blushed when he saw me coming into his store. I could never understand what he got all flustered about. Being the wife of a pharmacist was not in the cards for me — at least the cards that I was dealing to myself, much to my mother's dismay.

At the end of my first and only year of college, I applied to The American Musical and Dramatic Theater Academy in New York City. I would be in the second graduating class if I passed the audition. My audition was with Philip Burton (Richard Burton's foster father). The audition was simply to prepare one song to sing. They had an accompanist for the audition. I sang my song, adding a few dance moves, and that was really all there was to it. It surprised me the audition wasn't harder. Singing a song was easy for me. Whatever it was, I was accepted right on the spot, my heart almost burst with joy! This was probably an overreaction as it was a new school. They probably took any warm body with the tuition money! I didn't care! I was in! I walked out of the audition on cloud nine! As I walked down the school steps, all I could think about was that this was going to be my new home — Emerald City! Remembering the first time I saw New York City, I always referred to it as the Emerald City. I gazed up at the huge cranes that filled the sky with the power of future buildings in their grasp. That Christmas I actually bought cards with cranes on them with the New York sky line in the snow. When I was in junior high and took field trips to New York City, I always looked at the amazing skyline view with the blindingly beautiful high-rise buildings. The city looked like a jewel to me, that's why I called it Emerald City and I was following the yellow brick road to get there.

Walking down the city streets, dwarfed by the caverns of tall buildings, being part of the hustle of people watching, hurrying, striving to fulfill their dreams, I hardly felt my feet touch the ground. My heart was so vibrant and pumping so fast, I thought I may not make it back to Jersey. The sounds and smells and feel of this magnificent city and my monstrous success at my audition, filled me with an exhilaration past understanding. I can visualize and feel that moment anytime. Pure joy!

So I had gone from my porch productions, talent shows, school plays, to the big time in *the* big city! My dream was to study all the things I really loved all in one "school." No math, science, history for me. I was going to gorge myself on acting, singing and dancing. The mission of this new school was to train actors to be a *triple* threat. When you graduated from The American Musical and Dramatic Theater Academy, you would be at the zenith of your game in dance, voice, and drama. The entire program was only two years, so you had to work really hard to keep up with the competition. I immediately started looking for a place to live.

School was to start in two months. I found a brownstone apartment building on 3rd Avenue and 19th Street. It was called The Christian League for Woman. Rooms were nineteen dollars a month, including breakfast and dinner. My room was very small — a single bed, one window, a bureau and a closet. The bathroom was down the hall — shared by *everyone* on your floor. There were six tenants on my floor! I can still feel and see myself standing in that room barely large enough to turn around in. But this was my little room and mine alone! Being on my own was not like being in college or sleepover camp or even when I was in Europe on that tour.

I was truly on my own. I had to learn to make decisions. I learned to be a self-starter, get myself up, eat intelligently, (sure), find a job, use my time wisely, pay my bills, and study! Whew! I was all by myself in my own little home away from home. I'd never experienced that. I can remember my mother saying to me once, "Don't eat the whole candy bar or you'll be sick!" So I could never eat a whole candy bar. Silly I know. This was very disappointing. I was not the kind of daughter that was going to disobey her mother. I was afraid of her. I was afraid of my father. I was known as a very good girl — but I really wanted to eat that whole candy bar. I was in the subway one day. You can go all the way uptown in Manhattan (another word for NYC) by the subway train or all the way downtown, even one side to the other by switching subway trains. People also traveled by bus. Bus or subway, it's the easiest and cheapest way to get from one place to another, to the airport or to Coney Island for lots of summer fun. This particular day I was in the subway waiting for a train, I happened to notice a whole bunch of candy bars in a little booth where they also sold newspapers to people who were on their way to work. So as I passed by I noticed my very favorite candy bar, a Clark Bar. I bought one and of course, you know what I did — I ate the entire candy bar as fast as I could. I ate the whole candy bar just because I could do whatever I wanted. Unfortunately, my mother had been right. I felt so sick afterward, too much sugar, way too much sugar in such a short time, especially on an empty stomach. But I didn't care it was my choice. Funny the little things you remember when you were young and on your own. I returned to my little home away from home, my brownstone that had an old musty smell to it, a little stuffy, but so fun, so old New York City. Two elderly ladies were in charge of the boardinghouse. One funny thing I remember was a sign in the "parlor" stating, *No beaus allowed in the parlor after 10pm.* The parlor consisted of overstuffed couches and chairs. Magazines and books lay on a few small tables. Several floor lamps brightened the room. And of course, the windows were covered with thick draperies to keep people from looking in and you from looking out. My room window did have a nice view from the second floor. It overlooked a little park with benches and paths to the street. In the spring there were lots of flowers. The freedom I felt was nothing I had ever experienced. I had no fear of a classroom or being accepted by the people around me. I was just so happy. Ready to take on the world! Sometimes I wish I could just be there again, just a few days to capture that freedom once more, and the space of the world around me.

Since I had only asked my mom for tuition, I needed to find a job if I was to be able pay the rent. The ladies offered me a job serving dinner to the guests every evening. At breakfast that first morning there was a pretty blond girl serving the guests. We got chatting about moving to New York City — where are you from, that sort of thing, when we realized we were both going to the same acting school. Her name was Bonnie, beautiful little Bonnie from Chicago!

We both had to pay our way in the big city. So serving the guests at meal time would take care of some of our living expenses. Other jobs I would take on would be selling doughnuts in a local donut shop, ushering at a movie theater on 42nd street, and a hat check girl at the Village Vanguard. It was a jazz club at 7th Ave south of Greenwich Village. Sadly at the time I knew nothing about jazz. John Coltrane played there along with Miles Davis and many other famous Jazz musicians. Did I realize then how lucky I was? No. I just took hats and coats and came home smelling like a cigarette butt fiercely clutching my tips.

The donut shop partially doubled to provide some of my sustenance, although not very healthy, it was still food, as the owner always gave me leftover donuts. This added benefit would really come in handy when Bonnie and I moved in with one other girl from my school. They would eventually get jobs working there also.

As soon as I met these two girls from school I knew right away we had one important common desire — find a better place to live by sharing the rent and bring our cost of living down. These girls were to become my dearest friends for the rest of my life! Their problems were my problems. The love that developed between us is still strong to this day.

One of the girls from my school, Jo Ann, already lived in a fourth floor walk up Brownstone building with her roommate, Jennie. They needed more roommates to bring their rent down so Jo Ann asked Bonnie and me if we wanted to live with them. We said yes, but there was a minor problem, there were *four* girls and *three* beds. So the rule was — the last person in — slept on the couch.

The only person that ever happened to was Jennie. She had a boyfriend. He worked as a musician and played in a night club. She would hang out there till all hours. She was another beautiful brunette plus a talented writer. She and Jo Ann had the apartment originally. So Jennie felt really comfortable to just squeeze in bed with Jo Ann. Oh, sorry, I failed to mention that Jo Ann was a gorgeous brunette from the South. So when Jo Ann would wake up and find Jennie in bed with her, all wrapped around her, you would hear Jo Ann cry out in her southern accent, "Jennie Lo! What are you doin'? You are supposed to be on the couch!" This would happen almost every night. And every morning we would all laugh.

We were four fun loving girls with dreams to share, not realizing how fortunate we were having discovered each other at this time in this city.

We would be dubbed later in our lives, as "The 73rd street girls" by Bonnie, who would also write a play about us. You will see our photos on the next page. It really is sad we didn't take more pictures back then. We were just too busy trying to stay alive and get jobs.

My good friend, Bonnie, also wrote the introduction to my book.

OK, back to the "73rd street girls!"

Top left, young 73rd St. girls-Lanie, Bonnie and Jennie; upper right,
Jennie; mid right, Lanie and Jo Ann; lower right, Lanie and Bonnie;
lower left, young Jo Ann

Four girls in an apartment in the world's most fabulous city! What
more could you ask for at 20 years old? We were starving actresses just
like in the movies, only school was crazy awesome. So many kids from
everywhere wanting to become actors all so excited to be in New York.
Hustle, bustle, and tussle! That's what it was like. And on top of practicing
every day, we had to go to our jobs each night to pay the rent. I didn't

mind at all because I was on my own. I opened a bank account, which I knew nothing about, paid bills, wrote checks. I would call home, and say everything is just fine.

All of us quickly learned what the word "hunger" was all about. Day-old donuts didn't quite cut it. My dear old mom must have known. Very often she and my stepfather, George, would make a trip to the city with two large bags of groceries. When we heard them call at our window from down below on the street, we would race down the four flights of stairs to greet them. We would check out every item as fast as we could to see what they had brought this week. Then all of us would hug my mother and thank George. George was rather shy and always turned bright red. We would laugh and gently kiss him on the cheek then raced back up four flights with our newfound goods.

Here is a picture of my Mom and George, our personal food delivery service for the 73rd street girls.

I was kind of I relieved that they didn't want to walk up four flights of stairs to see our apartment. You can imagine what they would have thought. Three beds for four 20-year-old girls, clothing hanging up to dry surrounding the green refrigerator that was in the middle of the living room — they would pass through the kitchen on the way to the living room and not even notice it. For goodness sake! They never would have seen that coming. 1965 — that first year! What a fantastic year of fun and adventure! I wish I could give my mom and George a hug, now that I can appreciate them even more writing this book.

The most memorable adventure that year occurred on November 9, 1965 when the whole eastern seaboard, including parts of Canada, went dark! And when I say dark, I mean zero electricity anywhere! That's right, every single light, elevator, subway train in the city went *out of business*! I was on the subway when it happened. I was clueless, along with the passengers and I'm certain the operator and any of the conductors on the train. Picture this — dead stop — complete — and I mean complete darkness people becoming hysterical! And I was on my way to a new job as a waitress at a bar called Pal Joey's. To get there I started out at the west 79th Street entrance on Broadway and 7th Ave. This subway stop would take me down to the East Village, at least a half an hour ride. But not this particular night! I had a feeling I was in for big trouble.

We had no idea what was going on — or perhaps I should say not going on! After about 15 minutes of complete darkness amid frightened, wailing people, we heard a subway employee shouting, "Everyone move to the back of the train. We are going to vacate the train. We have no power. We will walk along the tracks until we get to the next station."

That's right we had come to a dead stop halfway to our next station. So here we were, all strangers, muttering and cursing and crying. Oh, yes, there is always someone who can't handle scary stuff — I will admit this was scarier than usual — and starts to think they are going to die. Walking down the subway rails was really a trip (no pun intended) guess who was wearing high heels? And I was all ready for my big chance as a waitress to earn lots of money — I was dressed to kill! But my attire really had no real significance because when we reached the street, we still had total darkness except for car headlights. The entire city was in an uproar. Everyone was scurrying frantically. Questions were being thrown around and answers were being thrown right back. No one knew anything except that there was no power. Let's just get out of here!

I couldn't call my new job because there was no electricity. (1965 — no cell phones either at this time.) I still had to get down to the Eastside somehow. I really needed that job. People were just jumping into cars that were stopping to help each other. Cabs were taking more than one passenger and not charging. Busses were bursting at the seams with hysterical people! I overheard someone shout from a car, "I am going to the eastside anybody need a ride?" I can still recall the darkness and chaos so vividly.

Thank goodness my mother was not there. You know she would have told me to walk, don't get into any stranger's car. Right, Mom, but these are unusual circumstances — understatement! And what she doesn't know won't hurt her. So I shouted back, "That's where I am headed. Can I hop in?" By the time the shouting was done there were four people in the back of the car and three in the front. After various stops for people closer than my lower Eastside stop, I finally arrived at Pal Joey's restaurant about 45 minutes later. So get this, I walk into a room aglow with candles, barely anyone there. The boss says to me, "Boy, I didn't think I would see you tonight! You must really want this job! I like that."

"Yes, well," I said. "This is my first night on the job and I wasn't going to let a little blackout stop me!"

"Well, sweetheart, it has stopped a lot of other people. We can't serve food so in a few minutes I'm going to close."

Now why didn't I think of that, my old over-conscientious self at work! No electricity in the entire city would mean everything was closing up. I was becoming a little uncomfortable because I appeared so clueless. Then one of the few patrons sitting alone at a candle-lit table called me over and said, "I couldn't help overhearing you and Bill talking."

"Yes, this was supposed to be my first night on the job. Some luck," I said.

"Bill, before you close will you pour me a gin and tonic and let the young lady at least serve one customer before she leaves. We don't want her to come down here for nothing. I am a fairly big tipper, you know."

I stood formally taking his order for his gin and tonic and he said, "You sure are pretty. I bet you're an actress. Am I right?"

Oh boy, I said to myself, here we go. I had been warned about lines like that to waitresses and in candlelight too! He said he was a producer and could probably get me into the movies. How original! Fortunately, my boss called me over and said he was closing because he felt the lights weren't coming on any too soon. No lights, no kitchen, no business. So I reported that news to my new *best friend* and I was out of there.

He followed me out and asked if he could give me a lift home.

"Thank you so much but I am meeting a couple of friends just around the corner." We both laughed nervously and parted.

"Oh, that's too bad. I thought we could go somewhere and talk about your career."

"That's very nice of you but not tonight."

Oddly enough I have no memory of ever working there again. I must have felt all that stuff about getting me into "pictures" was all too much. Give me a donut shop anytime!

I still had to get home and the darkness lingered. People were still frantically scurrying aimlessly to who knows where. Cars were trying to get out of town. Luckily I found another car that was filling up with people to help get them home, "Anyone going uptown?" Once again I got into a car with a stranger. (Mom you aren't listening right?) We all were one big mixture of people, rich, poor, young old, all with one thing in mind, how can we get home? It took a long time to get home because we all lived in so many different directions. Extraordinary patience was required that night. No one had any problem with that because we were all so glad that we were riding and not walking. As I watched the packed busses go by, I knew for sure I was really lucky.

People packed together in a bus meant only one thing if you were a woman. Some guy was going to try to grab your butt or rub against your back or front, or put a hand up your skirt or some other sexual imposition. And having been a recipient of much of that behavior on the subway, I was smiling gratefully as the buses rumbled by.

Finally I arrived at my destination, Broadway and 73rd Street. I gave the driver some money which he didn't want to take, but I insisted. As I closed the car door I noticed two Con Edison (the power company for the City of New York at that time) workers sitting on the steps of our building. I had to laugh how ironic here were two Con Ed employees aimlessly on my stoop the lights having been out for hours.

"What's up guys? What are you doing here? Aren't you supposed to be working or something?" I laughed a friendly laugh.

They laughed and said, "Yeah, yeah! Very funny! Very funny!"

"Well you see," the short guy said as he tipped his hat, "We are in the same boat with a million other people. We can't get home! Trains aren't running as you know, and we live on the island." (Long Island)

"So you have no place to stay?"

"All the hotels are full and too expensive anyway. We figure we will just lay low here until morning. By then let's hope the electricity is back on. We'll just go back to work at our office."

I always knew I had inherited my mother's soft spot for anybody who was in trouble to always try to *lend a hand*. Consequently, you guessed it. I felt sorry for the two men and said, "You can come up to my apartment and sleep on the floor or whatever." I am not sure I would do that today but you never know!

Out of the corner of my eye I spotted a mattress just down the block on the sidewalk leaning against a tree. You have to really love New York. You can find anything you really need simply by looking up and down the block, on sidewalks or down the local ally. So there the three of us were, walking up four flights of stairs to my apartment. Oh, yes, did I mention that they were carrying the mattress? When I opened the door, I noticed my two roommates were sleeping. I showed the two Con Edison workers the living room and said, "Hope you two sleep well."

Thanks, was all they said, except that they would be out early and take the mattress with them. One took the mattress, the other hit the couch — and I panicked! Good grief what if Jennie comes home? What in the world had I done? The good news — Jennie did not come home that night. A 20-year-old female scream — would have no trouble reaching the first floor! I am still whipping my brow.

Morning came quickly because I didn't get home until 2 AM. The early sun streaming through the bedroom window woke me up. Maybe I never even slept. I am really not sure. At any rate a big grin came over my face and my hand waved, as the two men walked by the bedroom carrying the mattress and mouthing, thank you! I think my mother and George, if they had found out, would wonder if my next naïve stunt could be any worse!

I thought I had done such a lovely thing so I told my roommates all about it.

I forget who but one of them said, "Lanie, let me get this straight — you invited two strange men up to sleep in our apartment. You then found a mattress on the street for them to carry upstairs so they would be comfortable. Did you forget — three attractive 20-year-old females were waiting upstairs? No way, no way!"

I could only shrug. Well, I guess, it was quite shocking when I started to really think about it. (I continue to do that sort of thing but that's another book) I was starting to feel embarrassed so

I just said, "Okay, I was kidding because the whole night was so impossible, I thought I would add a little drama." They just couldn't believe I would do such a thing! We all laughed and that was that. Over the years every once in a while someone will say where were you when we had the blackout? There were going to be a lot more unbelievable things that were going to happen in the big city. And I had 40 more years there to experience *all* of them.

The photos below are from – *My Fair Lady*, *The Sound of Music*, Princess Ella, a commercial picture, lower left – me signing an autograph (My husband found and bought that picture on line for $25! He is such a fan!) Next- *My Fair Lady* The next photo was from the Charles Theatre in Boston.

One of my first auditions that year was an open-call for a summer stock company that was going to tour the summer theater tents with the latest musicals. After waiting an hour my name was called. Briefly into my audition, the director stopped me from singing. He said he couldn't believe his luck in finding me. He then offered me the leads in two of the four musicals. I was stunned! There was even more good fortune — the company was already an Equity company. When they hired me, I automatically and immediately became a union member and secured my union card. I later found out that some actors wait years for their card. At the time I had no idea how lucky I was. The experience was past marvelous. Singing and dancing in all the shows I loved having seen on Broadway, *My Fair Lady* and *Oklahoma*. One of my leading men was the actor I played opposite in when I was in *The Boy Friend,* in college. He was the person who introduced me to the acting school. He had already graduated. We really worked well together. He was to become a good friend. He was a lot older and led me by the hand when I got too "full of myself." I was to return another year and tour with the same producer and director, with more leads one being, *The Sound of Music*.

Remember when my mother got a call from my acting teacher in New York asking her if I could be in the chorus of the Broadway production *Bye-Bye Birdie*. My mother, doing her job as she should, said no a 15-year-old girl could not go in and out to New York City by herself — especially at night. She was right. Except when you are 15 and in love with New York City and Broadway shows, and you could have been in a Broadway show — **NO,** cannot possibly be the right answer.

Fast forward five years and I was saying Hi-Hi Lanie to the show *Bye-Bye Birdie*! I auditioned for a Summer Stock Theater and got the lead in *Bye-Bye Birdie* and three other hit musicals of the times. So five years later I traded a part of the chorus for the lead! As you will discover, things got better and better from there. I was one of the fortunate 20-year-old small-town girls in New York City trying to make a big.

Such was the beginning of my acting career in the big city of New York. I was to have many wonderful times with the actors and actresses that walked the pavements looking for work.

Top left - Summer stock tour. It looks a little scary. *My Fair Lady*,
top right. That production used the same costumes as the movie
with Audrey Hepburn. Needless to say I was in heaven wearing those
dresses. Not to mention — that white hat!

Lower left - *Oklahoma* Lower right - *Can Can* I was in the chorus.
More photos can be seen on IMDb website, just type in my name.

CHAPTER 7
My First Love

I was 21 when I enrolled in the American Musical and Dramatic Theater Academy in New York City. This school offered acting, singing, and
dancing instruction as musicals were very big in that era — the idea was
to graduate as a triple threat! As I walked into my first acting class, there
was Michael a lovely boy about my age. Our eyes locked as I sat down next
to him. We sat there with our eyes touching each other until our spell was
broken by the mellow voice of our instructor. The rest of the class laughed
gently, understandingly. So began my first true love. A boy and a girl in
New York City, two would-be stars, — two country bumpkins with no
knowledge of the city or life in general, fell in love. One thing we knew
for sure, we were into something good!

We started slow this was in 1962 before the big sexual revolution,
everyone using the Internet to go out on a date which meant "hooking-up."
We spent a year studying and preparing for the Broadway Theater, and a
year of kissing — period. We both lived in downtown Manhattan. I lived
at The Friendly League for Christian Women. Michael had an apartment
with a roommate from school.

It had been almost two years of studying and excitement. One night
we were studying at his apartment. I said, "It's getting late and I am getting

a little tired, I should be going back to my place." Michael said, "Why don't you stay over?"

"Well, I don't know." I fidgeted a little bit. "I'd just like to lie down for a while but then I better go because, remember, the old ladies who run our boarding house lock the doors at 10 PM sharp." So we both lay down on Michael's bed for a little rest.

Then something very strange happened. We started kissing, and I guess we got most of our clothes off, because all I can remember is that — we were kissing and something hard on Michael's body just slipped into me. I know it's difficult for you to believe as you read this. Yes, apparently my mother fell short in this aspect of raising me, and I was completely unaware of what was happening. Shocking I know, but sadly true.

I did get up, got dressed and kissed Michael goodbye, neither one of us saying anything about anything. It was one of those "it never happened" moments. My problem was that I didn't understand what the "it never happened" moment was. What really *did* happen?

It's obviously no secret to you now but I will say it out loud — I was completely clueless about sex! Somehow I had avoided or missed out on any discussion of it with other girls during my years in school. I know my mother just gave me a book on the Birds and Bees. I found out later that almost all of the girls in college had explored and experimented with their bodies in puberty. But me? I never had the inclination. This was years before anybody taught sex education in elementary or high school. Sex education was the unspoken job of parents in those days. Apparently that fact was lost on my mother. In my 18 years living with her before college, we never *ever* talked about sex at any time. I realized years later the complete void in the area of sex in my life was the reason I was frightened in my early encounters with my father. My fear was totally intuitive, not based on any kind of learned knowledge. At this point in my life and up until my mid-70s, sitting on my father's lap still haunted me.

Walking from Michael's back to my boarding house, the incident on my father's lap crept into my mind. I still couldn't see his face. Why couldn't I see his face? Did my intuitive frightened feeling and conse-quential paralysis of my arm have anything to do with my blocking out the look on his face? All I remember is that I was always uncomfortable around my father.

I can say I thought I was in love with Michael. But I have to admit I wasn't really sure what love was. And I was always uncomfortable around Michael as well. I think I was generally afraid of men for a long time before I discovered my sexuality. I was confused about the role men were supposed to play in my life, sexually, and the role I was supposed to play, sexually, in theirs. And not being familiar with sexual feelings at all — presented a real problem for me. If my sexual feelings were blocked, and I was *afraid* to unlock them, what then was I suppose to do?

At any rate, I'm walking back to my place, and all I realized was that "it slipped in." I just made it to the boarding house entrance as Miss Hamilton already had her key inserted in the lock.

"Well, just in the nick of time, Miss Norton," she frowned.

Sensing her disappointment, I said, "Yes, Miss Hamilton!" huffing and puffing as if I had run all the way — I hope she knew I was making fun of her. "I guess I just made it in the nick of time!"

The following morning I was to cross paths with Michael on the way to school. As he approached me on the sidewalk, I could see this look of wonder on his face, the gleaming smile in his eyes (I will never forget that look) as he walked with an extra hop in his step. It's as if he was gliding over the sidewalk. He was an amazing dancer, and so perhaps he was reliving last night with his little light hop and skip and jump kind of dance. His eyes were beaming with the glow of something I had never seen from a male. As we got closer, my intuition, reminded me that I was supposed to know something, some wonderful secret that he wanted to share with me.

Dear me, sadly I felt no hop, skip, or jump in my step. I don't think there was even as much as a gleam in my eyes. Nevertheless, I felt Michael's need for me to respond to his dance and his glow in a particular way — I was totally clueless. Wait a minute, I thought, I am an actress! I can act my way through this. I broke into a big smile and took his hand rather lovingly, and knowingly looked into his eyes trying to match his apparent joy of last night.

As we walked hand-in-hand, I felt nothing! No romantic bliss. No love as I understood it really. All I knew was that something had slipped into me — so? We continued on to our acting class. No word was ever spoken about our evening together.

Photo from the Children's Theater Company — at the Charles Playhouse in Boston

Michael and I had just graduated from the Academy. We went to an open call for the Charles Playhouse in Boston. The theater wanted to start a Saturday morning children's theater company. We were to perform original musicals. It was a one season job. We decided we could take the job if offered and live together in Boston. As you can see in the picture above, we were hired! The prospect of living unmarried with Michael was very exciting although taboo in those days. My mother made her feelings known by writing her thoughts down, about how we were shamefully living together, and then mailing them. Another comment in her letters was, "Well, I wonder what the mailman is thinking today while delivering a letter to my daughter, who is living with a man in Boston she's not married to?" Or how about this — "Lanie, I see you as a white dove being dragged through the mud. (That's a vivid memory.) Can't you please come home?" I shrugged off my mother's negativity determined to move my career forward.

When our show closed in Boston, I could no longer live with Michael. We loved performing in the theatre but unfortunately our relationship in a word — strained! My love for him was not being returned in a fashion I could understand. At this point, I still didn't have any clue of a male-female relationship regarding romance and love. Michael was at a loss to understand why I wasn't happy.

The upshot was Michael stayed in Boston, and I went back to New York City — crying hard, most of the bus trip from Boston. Leaving Michael was the most difficult decision I had made in my life so far. Especially when I wasn't sure what was wrong! Riding the bus back to New York I had that feeling once again I was not *being seen*. Michael was all about living and I was all about wanting to be loved. Later, I realized that it's very difficult to be *seen* when you have trouble *seeing* yourself! The passionate love that I thought I had for Michael slowly and painfully dried up and died. We would never see each other again.

CHAPTER 8

I Need Help

As I got off the bus from Boston, my emotions reached a level unfamiliar to me. Leaving Michael was confusing and devastating. I reached my apartment that I was sharing with two new girls. Where were my old friends from 73rd St.? I'm guessing off on adventures as I had been. I sure could have used their friendship about now. I sat staring out the window overlooking the night lights of Manhattan. What do I do now? I was not feeling well physically or psychologically. No one to talk to! What was the matter with me?

The next thing I knew I was standing on the Eastside overpass staring into the water. How did I get here — better question — what was I doing here? Did I want to jump and splash bang, kill myself? I had hit bottom! I had cried all the way from Boston to New York when losing Michael, but I was the one who left him. Was I still haunted by my father thinking I was worthless? Had that played a part in my relationship with Michael? No answers and jobless there I was staring into the dark waters, not to mention my mother was urging me to come home and marry the phar-macist. (That would definitely make me jump!) Somehow nothing was left to live for! We've all been there! I was looking down into the river, dark and foreboding, wondering what in the world I was doing there. What in the world was I doing anywhere? My knees gave out and I collapsed into a lump against the bridge guard rail, sobbing.

I can't say if I really heard this or I was telling it to myself, as a car drove by. I heard a voice say, "Don't do it lady, life is not that bad!" I jerked around to see who had yelled it and managed a smile. I could suddenly see myself, this miserable lump of human being, considering suicide and shook my head almost to shake me out of this state of nonsense. Those words struck me where I lived. Come on, I am 23 something — I am going to have more love affairs and probably have more broken hearts. I had only been out of work maybe, one day! I mean really, Lanie. Get a grip! Just find someone to talk to. You have a life to live! Somehow, and I'll never know for sure, I had returned to my apartment, sat down on my bed when something struck me! I thought to myself this is not how I want to feel. Feeling sad hurts too much! I want to be happy. I clearly remember that moment of choosing happiness. That choice of happiness brought me around to reality. I was just starting out, got my first job at a well known theater in Boston and still in my early 20s! What's not to be happy about?

No need to jump, but maybe the need to find out why I was standing there in the first place. I decided to call a friend I had met through my roommates from school. He was studying to be a psychologist. I called him and told him what had happened. How I found myself wanting to jump off the East River Bridge! He told me definitely I needed to get some professional help. I said thanks, and found a psychologist, Dr. Ryan, in the phone book. (Remember those days?) Little did I realize at the time he was to be my next romantic encounter.

In those days going to a therapist meant you were crazy in the head. Of course now, if you aren't seeing a shrink, you must be crazy in the head. At any rate I was going. Always moving forward, that's for me. Pick yourself up, dust yourself off, and start all over again! I sang that song at my high school talent show. So I took it to heart. You do a lot of starting over in the acting business.

I made an appointment and found myself on the bus to my first therapy session. As I sat there, I could feel my hands getting very clammy. When I looked down to check the address — for the third time — my fist was so tight I could barely open my hand. When I did, my sweaty hand opened up to reveal a wet crumpled up piece of paper I could barely read. When I reached my stop, I jumped up, pulled the cord, and jumped off. (You have to get off fast before the driver starts up again. They have a schedule to keep!) I walked searching for the building numbers on the brownstones. As I walked, I looked up the long steps to the various buildings trying to read the addresses. There it was! I'm here. I walked up the steps. Now I had to find his name and office number. I was having no luck quieting my nerves. I was going to be talking to a total stranger. Not small talk either. He would ask me to share my most intimate thoughts, my innermost secrets and hidden fears. When I thought about it my innermost thoughts and hidden fears were not easily deciphered. There it was a small white strip of paper, Dr. Ryan, and a buzzer. I buzzed to let him know I was outside. After a short while the door buzzed back. I entered the building. His office was on the second floor. Brownstone buildings can have as many as five flights. Like the one I lived in with the 73rd St. girls. Was I thankful I had to walk up merely two flights, two creaky flights with no light, with a very musty smell? Am I really going in there? I wavered and started to turn around. Too late — the office door opened and a man said, "Lanie Norton?" I nodded yes. "Come in please, pleasure to meet you. I'm Dr. Ryan."

Thinking back I could have said, "Oh, sorry. I am just coming to visit a friend down the hall. Pardon the ring." Alas, instead, you can see, I walked in.

Dr. Ryan was 40ish, stood a little under 6-foot, was slight of build, had curly salt and pepper hair with beady eyes piercing through oversized glasses. He must have been concerned about his being thin. His suit was so over-sized it looked like his body had been draped over a hanger, his head and hands added as an afterthought. There was an uncomfortable silence as we looked at each other over his desk. I broke it with, "So what do we do now?"

"Why don't you lie down over there on the couch," he answered.

"What did you say?" He spoke in a very quiet tone so I had to ask him to repeat himself. Being an actress and having the first thing someone tells me to do, especially a male in his office, is to lie down on the couch, didn't sit too well with me. A male agent wanted me in a slip one time to see if I could still act. Duh! However, this was my first therapist. I was still dressed. I did what he asked and lay down on the couch. He sat behind his desk with a notepad. He asked me what I would like to talk about.

So my first therapy session began. I relaxed some and began to talk. I went immediately to the scary thing I had done at the bridge. Breaking up with Michael took away my reason for living. I didn't jump, but I needed to get myself back on track in my life. I needed somebody to tell me that breaking up with someone you were "forever going to be in love with" happened all the time with everyone. We talked a lot about how this might happen again as part of reality with male-female relationships. I was young and this being my first serious love interest, it was very natural to feel confusion. We also talked about what my father had done to me. This haunting of not being able to see his face was something I really wanted to discuss and dispel. So the next couple of sessions I lay on the couch, I told him at 5 years old I paralyzed my arm and I don't know how it happened.

"Were you under stress?" He asked.

"I don't know."

"Where were you when it happened?"

"I was sitting on my father's lap. We were tickling each other, I think. I can't remember."

"At anytime did he grab your arm and hold it really tight?"

"I don't think so," I said.

"Maybe you were really roughhousing a little with him and don't remember."

"No, we were not doing that. I was just sitting on his lap facing him."

"What was his expression as you were sitting on his lap?"

Oh boy, here we go. What was I going to say? I should remember what he looked like, right? But I just can't remember. How would this doctor help me remember that?

"Well, you see that's the problem," I said.

"What's the problem?" I could not answer.

"Tell me what your relationship with your father was like."

"Really, we had no relationship that I can remember. That moment on his lap is the first time I can remember being with my father, I was only 5 years old."

"You were pretty little at the time but five is old enough to remember some things. What is the next memory of your father? Did he seem concerned with your paralyzed arm?"

"On the contrary, he never asked me to sit on his lap ever again and it was never spoken of."

Dr. Ryan sat there quietly thinking. I could see him writing in his book. He looked up.

"Well, Lanie, from what you have described to me and the length of time you have spent trying to remember what happened, I would say you were traumatized in some way at that early age of five.

"How was I traumatized?"

"Well, that's another problem we would have to look into. If you were traumatized, you could have possibly experienced conversion disorder."

"What is that?"

"When you were sitting on your father's lap, you may have unknowingly experienced, a traumatic event and your body responded by paralyzing your arm. Actually any part of your body can be paralyzed when experiencing stress or trauma, but for you it was your arm that was paralyzed."

"What kind of stress could I have experienced?"

"This is what we will try to uncover in our sessions."

Not being sure of what he was saying, left me even more confused.

My sessions continued for weeks. Talking with a complete stranger in semi-darkness, who could not make eye contact, was I really going to find out why my arm was paralyzed? Doubtful.

Oddly, at the end of one session he handed me a plant. I asked, "What is this for?" He stuttered slightly and said, "I just want to give you something."

I was so obviously flattered I felt my face flush. He cracked a shy smile. I had never seen him smile since we started working together. His face was actually a gray cloud and would work well for an FBI agent. I thought no more about the gift until the next session.

At this session, he kept me past my session time. When I finally questioned him about the other times he kept me overtime, he said, "Not a problem for you to concern yourself with."

After the following session, he stopped me as I was leaving, and blurted out, "I think we should go out on a date." The only noise in the room was our loud breathing. I was stunned! What did he just say? He was my therapist! What happened to all that professionalism and Hippocratic Oath stuff?

Flushed and confused, I responded by saying, "A patient doesn't go out with their therapist!" I gave him one last glare, turned and quickly left.

Let me interject that I don't feel it is appropriate or even a good idea for a patient to date their therapist. Even so, I know it goes on all the time in our culture. At the time, however, I trusted Dr. Ryan. I saw him as a possible father figure, as a god. He was going to help me. I was still concerned about the obvious lack of professionalism on his part. I spent the whole next week going back and forth in my mind as to what to do. I rationalized that he and I came from different perspectives and this might be something I should do. After all this is his profession. Wait a minute this is beginning to feel familiar. Did I say father figure? I was ambivalent with my father and now I am being ambivalent with Dr. Ryan. What's going on? Oh make a choice Lanie! Okay I'll go out with him.

When I went back for my following session, the door to his office was already open. He called from his office to come in. He was sitting at his desk head down, pretending to work. I broke the silence with, "I thought a lot about what you said, Dr. Ryan. Okay, let's go out on a date." It was his turn to be flushed in the face. He couldn't look me in the eye. He continued to fidget with papers at his desk still unable to look at me. I was dumbfounded. Here I was expecting a hug or maybe, that's great or something positive, yet...?

He told me he was sorry, but he was really busy this summer and, as a matter of fact, he wouldn't be able to go out with me until — December or so.

"December ..... Did he just say December?" My jaw dropped in wonderment! There was a long uncomfortable silence — hands all quiet on his desk, eyes still not meeting mine! "If I can't see you until December, what were you doing asking if you could date me last week? It's April for heaven's sake. Now you're telling me maybe December... maybe, December!" He said nothing, while looking at his hands sheepishly. I could tell he was uncomfortable. Maybe he knew it was wrong.

Somehow he managed to reduce himself even farther down into his oversized suit, still not answering me. I continued to stare at him for at least a minute longer.

I spoke, "I don't know what's going on here but something is wrong. I may have to go to someone else to find out what just happened here because I'm really confused!" I slammed the door on my way out.

I was just putting my purse down as I arrived at my apartment. The phone rang. It was Dr. Ryan!

"Excuse me! What are you doing calling me?"

"Are you really serious about having to talk to somebody else about what just happened?"

"Of course, I'm serious! And, of course, I'm going to have to talk to somebody else!" There was anger in my voice. "What kind of person or therapist are you to do this to a patient?"

You are not going to believe what he answered — "Well I have the name of a therapist for you to call. He's a friend of mine. He could help you."

My confusion mounted, my anger rose. Wanting to end this, rather exasperated, I answered, "Fine. What's his name and number?"

"Great, that's fine," I hung up.

The following day I called this Dr. Jones and made an appointment. I went to see him a couple of days later. Those few days I waited to see my new therapist were confusing and somehow frightening. After all, Dr. Jones and Dr. Ryan were friends, had he already told him my/our story? It was crazy.

I went to the appointment. I can still see the man shaking his head when I told him what had happened. Of course, he ethically couldn't talk trash about his friend, another therapist. What he told me was these sorts of problems can occur between a patient and a therapist — it's called transference. I must have looked at him blankly because he proceeded to explain what transference was. I was still trying to figure out what trauma caused my conversion disorder, whatever that meant! He told me sometimes in therapy, because of the intense emotional content of the session, a situation can evolve where one transfers his emotional feelings to the other — either patient or therapist or both could do this. If one or the other is in need of some kind of sexual/love relationship, it is easy for the transference to occur.

"So you're telling me Dr. Ryan fell in love with me?"

"Simply put, yes."

How could you fall in love with someone in the dark, you only see once a week? I am still shaking my head at that one. I had a couple more sessions with Dr. Jones, I noticed the lights were on, — no transferences. Thank goodness!

Unfortunately, before my next session, I had an audition for a pre-Broadway show and was hired for the part. Therapy was going to have to wait. The part was to understudy the lead, a celebrity singer at the time. I was thrilled to get the job. The lead understudy on a huge pre-Broadway summer stock tour is what every ambitious actress dreams of. The opportunities this job could offer me were endless!

Yes, this job was great, but was I emotionally ready? A new and significant challenge in my life brought much anxiety. I wasn't even close to beginning to deal with why I was so depressed after I left Michael, and how to resolve that eye-opening night on the bridge. Not to mention my therapist falling in love with me, then rejecting me! What is going on? Even so, does anything ever keep an actress from taking a job? You know the answer to that one.

CHAPTER 9
Broadway Understudies

I am sitting on the tour bus for a pre-Broadway musical. This production was touring the United States to prepare for Broadway. I am almost sick with excitement and fear. I look around the bus to see who is with me. I have seen some of these faces on auditions, so I guess we are some of those who did not get rejected, at least for this job. I look down at the man sitting next to me. He is wearing a wedding ring. The bus door closes. I can hear the gears engaging and the bus starts moving out of New York City. I am watching out the window as the 50-foot canyons of buildings get smaller and smaller leaving my city.

We have been on the road for about half an hour when the married man next to me turns to me, "Would you like to hook-up on the tour?"

"Excuse me? What do you mean hook-up?"

"You know — share a room on the tour."

"I'm looking directly at your wedding ring. You want me to hook-up with a married man?"

"Well that's not really a problem for me."

"Sorry, but it really is a problem for me." I returned my attention out the window.

I could see that my social education was going to be extended, at least in the entertainment business. The next time I got on the bus I learned something else. When I looked down this time, his wedding ring was gone. So, I thought to myself, that's how it works, when a married man wants to go to bed with a strange woman, don't broadcast you're a married man.

I had learned things about the male-female sexual relationship among actors who tour. I was now going to learn some new things about the female-female sexual relationship. This learning came from being in the chorus as well as the understudy to the lead. What is an understudy? The main characters in a production may encounter situations that keep them from performing, — fat chance of that happening. Therefore each of them needs an understudy. Just as the lead has to learn her part, I have to learn her part as well, so that I can go on stage when the need arises. I have to learn the cues, the lines, the songs, the blocking and the choreography. In other words I have to be her shadow. In my later experiences, I learned that leads are not always happy to work with their understudies. Consequently, they make learning the part and other aspects of the performance difficult.

I lucked out as my lead and I became friends. After hours, we spent a lot of time together eating and drinking and getting to know each other. Things were going well, until I was approached by someone in the chorus who was gay. I had no idea she was gay. I didn't even know what gay meant. When I was around her, she would just start flirting with me, pushing and shoving, laughing, taking her hand and tussling with my hair! It was like she was friendly, but somehow more than that. I admit my intuition told me something was not quite right. I said to myself, what is going on with her? Her messing around made me nervous. The actors were always looking at us. I was having a good time being with her. What was I nervous about?

The next time I got on the bus one of the guys behind me said, "You know, Lanie, there's a lot of talk around that you're gay. Are you?"

"Gay? No."

"Come on, Lanie! Connie has made it clear that she wants you around her. Breakfast in the cafeteria, lunch on the set, drinks after rehearsal. We all know she's gay. If you're not, what the heck are you doing spending all that time with her?"

"What are you talking about? She is just being friendly and fooling around with me. She likes me. And I like her. We're becoming good friends."

What was the big deal? I didn't tell them I didn't understand what gay meant, but it didn't matter to me. I liked her for who she was when she was with me. Isn't that how it is suppose to be? Labels, I was not a fan of labels.

"You're telling us you're not gay. Seriously? If you're not gay, why don't you hang out with us for a while? We're good looking guys raring to go show you a good time. You are a beautiful, talented and smart actress. Why don't you want to have a good time with us? Try us out for a change. See if you don't think we have more to offer than your chorus friend."

There I was with all these male minds offering me, a supposedly young gay woman, a chance to turn her head around to become heterosexual. I tell you it was quite a disturbing mess that I never saw coming. I was still trying to figure out what happened in the shrink's office. No one really aroused me sexually among these loud-mouth guys. On top of all this, some of the girls pretended to be gay just so the guys would try to sleep with them. So when the girls got together, they were always laughing about how they fooled the guys into thinking that would make a difference. I was really spacey that whole trip. I didn't know whether I was coming or going. It didn't mess up my performance but I had definitely had trouble relating to the actors.

One of the actresses asked if I wanted to ride with her as she had her own car. Well, you can imagine, I jumped at the chance to get away from the guys on the bus. The conversation during the ride was pleasant until she brought up the topic of me being gay. Why is everyone so interested in me being gay? I confirmed yet again that I was not gay. I asked her why she was interested in whether I was gay or not. I never imagined what her response was going to be. She started to pour out her deepest secret.

"You know," she said, "I have always been curious about…"

"About what…?" I asked. She struggled to share her thoughts with me and then the bomb was dropped.

"Would you like to experiment with me and see what it's all about?"

I can still see myself sitting in the car speechless. By now I was starting to be sorry I was even on the tour. I really didn't know what she was talking about. Experiment how? I was so clueless about most things. She was a beautiful red head, what did she want with me? What do I say? There was silence in the car, I better say something. The only thing I could think of was to tell her she wasn't my type. She didn't say a word. I don't really know what I meant by that, but I wasn't interested in whatever she wanted. I felt lost and stupid sitting there in her car. She was quiet for the rest of the trip. I must have embarrassed her.

Maybe the bus wasn't so bad after all.

A few weeks into the tour I experienced a man wanting to "hook up" with me via fan mail. I was getting fan mail in my own tiny dressing room! The problem was this fan was anonymous. Anonymous fan letters are good news and bad news. Good news, because it's fun to have fans — bad news because I have somebody maybe stalking me! I was getting letters from a particular fan telling me how beautiful I was. How talented I was. I was not ready for this first time fan crush or how to confront this situation. During one performance, as I danced down the aisle toward the stage, (the understudies are always in the chorus), I looked around trying to spot the gentleman who had eyes for me.

I didn't have to wait very long as my mystery fan quickly introduced himself to me. He was a man in the orchestra. He knocked on my door and visited me in my dressing room to express his fondness for me. He was very attractive. I had learned something about sex. Especially that I was heterosexual. I decided to go out with him after the show. The change would do me good. At that time we all resided in the same hotel. He suggests we go to his room for a drink first. I gave him a friendly nod and off we went. Back at his hotel room, we start to kiss — it starts to get heated. He breaks it off. "You know, I'm so sorry I just can't. I am Catholic and married."

Oh no, here we go again. What's up with this guy! "You are Catholic and married. So why did you invite me to your room?" No comment. "How would I know you are married? The point is if you are married, what are you doing asking me for a date? Do I look like the kind of woman that enjoys helping men commit adultery?" He stood here with his mouth open. By now I have had it with gays, want to be gays, married men and heterosexuals. I gathered up my belongings, and walked out. I did not love this part of the tour.

Looking back, even after all my previous whining, on the whole, I have to admit I loved the experience. I met a lot of fun people. I learned how to deal with people in terms of sexual relations. Unfortunately, this show and I were never to reach Broadway.

But another show was about to present itself, and possibly give me another chance at the "brass ring!" Several weeks later I received a call from Honey, my agent.

"Well dear," she said, "you have another Broadway audition."

"What? What are you talking about?"

"There is a new Broadway show in the works. I am sending you to audition for the lead ingénue understudy."

"What is the show about?"

"It is called *Angel*. It is taken from the book, *Look Homeward Angel*. It's a musical. It will star Fred Gwynne, from *The Munsters*. There is a young girl in the cast. You are auditioning for her understudy" Understudy's I know about and I can handle it.

Honey told me all the details for the audition and wished me luck. I was excited to have another opportunity to be on Broadway. I was ready for it. I loved auditioning. I would see my friends up for the same part. We would all wonder who would get it this time. After the audition we would talk about who got what lately — did you see so and so in whatever? Always wishing it had been us to get that part.

It was time, I was up next. They gave me a script to read from. A woman assistant to the director read opposite me as my love interest. The reading went well. I heard, "Thank you. Are you working at the moment?" What did I say? That's right — "No I am between jobs at the moment."

"Would you be able to come in tomorrow to read with the actor auditioning for the male understudy?"

"Yes I can do that. What time would you like me to come in?"

"I will call your agent. She will be in touch. Thank you for coming in."

"Thank you." As I left the stage and walked back through the waiting room, the other girls asked, "How did it go?" You always give them a noncommittal answer. They always respond with, "Good luck!" You always hope you did well and the part is yours. They called me back to audition the next day. I read with an actor that was up for the male understudy opposite me. He wasn't anyone I had seen at auditions before, but we read well together. It was a love scene and I got to be very romantic. Funny, I could do love scenes on stage really well, but in real life?

"Thank you. We will let you know."

The final auditions were in two days. I received another call to return. There I was again, paired up with the same actor I had read with before. This was a good sign. I had to believe they liked how we worked together and looked together. My hopes were really high. After the audition, the director asked us if we were available to start work next week if they wanted us. We both quickly answered, "Yes!" Then we looked at each other and laughed!

The director said, "Now let's not get ahead of ourselves," and smiled. "I will be in touch with your agents. Next please, Maria!"

We left the stage trying "not to get ahead of ourselves!" You can imagine my excitement when Honey called the next day with a, "You got it kid!" Honey Raider, was the best and most positive agent in New York. She was my agent all through the years.

So there I was rehearsing my lines with the same actor I read with. We were both understudies, but who cared? Finally, I was going to open on Broadway!

Wrong again! After 5 days on Broadway, the critics squashed it. Oddly enough some of the leads received Broadway awards! What's wrong with this picture?

Broadway and me, were not meant to be! (Sorry for the rhyme.)

CHAPTER 10
Apartment Superintendent?

Two years of summer stock tours and a few other acting jobs, one being a puppeteer for Jim Henson, (My arm was so sore, I couldn't hail a cab for weeks!) offered me a chance to rent my own apartment. There was a living room, kitchen, bedroom, and bathroom. A solid gold find in New York City. I accomplished this feat knowing a friend who knew a friend who knew a friend — you know the drill. My apartment was on the second floor of a brownstone at 79th and Broadway. (Brownstone buildings in New York City are like townhouses with steps leading up to the front door.) Only $100 a month! (You don't see that anymore!)

As I was leaving the building one day, Jerry, a young man from the first floor apartment, stopped me to talk for a moment. He and his girlfriend had lived there for about a year and were leaving. He said he was surely going to miss his free rent. Why was he telling me this? He told me he was the superintendent and now the building owner was going to have to find a new one. Jerry knew everyone in the building and no one wanted to be the new superintendent. He said he didn't know me very well and maybe I would want to be the new superintendent and get free rent. What are the responsibilities? He said you are in charge of the building. You will have to fix leaky sinks and clogged toilets. You will need to collect the garbage every week. Mop floors, make sure hall lights are on that kind of thing. I told him there was nothing there that I could not do. Please tell the owner I was very interested. A few weeks later, I had my free rent on my second floor brownstone apartment — could I be any luckier! My mom was going to be so excited to know that now my New York life included cleaning toilets, fixing sinks, mopping floors, and collecting garbage.

The owner came around to show me the building, and give me some instructions. We walked from the boiler room to the top floor. I now had two jobs, being an actress — and being the superintendent of an apartment building with 16 tenants. You see, there is nothing I won't try. Nothing!

The owner told me that if there was anything I had questions about to ask, Luigi, the superintendent across the street. I met Luigi. He was 65 and one of those salt of the earth people. We got along famously. I loved his Italian accent. We were talking one day as fall was turning to winter. He said, "*Leone, hey, loo-ka ovah dere. We gotta beega sno-stor comin'.*" At first I didn't understand. Then I realized another one of my superintendent responsibilities was to shovel the walk for my building, notice I said my building. I really had no idea where my walk stopped. I decided I would just wait until all the superintendents got out there shoveling, and I would know where my walk stopped.

I got up the next morning to see a foot of snow on the sidewalks, steps and stoop. With great enthusiasm, I got right to it. No foot of snow was going to get me down. I was going to go out and play in the snow with all the other superintendents!

This was heavy East Coast snow. As I shoveled, I took off my winter coat because of the perspiration. Luigi called to me from across the street. "*Hey, Leone, yu shova da sno dow-na-hil, notta uppa Hil!* He was kind of laughing and pointing. I must have been doing something wrong. The buildings in that area were on a small hill. I realized I was starting at the bottom of the hill and pushing the snow *uppa hil* that's what he was talking about. Some of the other superintendents who were shoveling their side walks, stopped and laughed a little. So I went to the top of my walk and started shoveling snow *dow-na hil!* I felt a little silly, but yelled back laughing, "Thanks!" We were all superintendents shoveling our first snow of the season, *dow-na hil!*

All superintendents in my neighborhood were male. I was female, young, and attractive, and I came in contact with everyone in my building. My first job as superintendent inside the building was a call from Andy, a male tenant in his early 30's, very single, very lost. He said he was having trouble with his kitchen sink. I came to fix it. All he needed was a washer. It was easy. On my way out of his apartment, he wanted to know if I had time to see some of his slides, pictures of his vacation in Philadelphia. (Philadelphia?) These kinds of requests from young males and old males were becoming old hat for me. Andy was always waiting with an ear pressed to his door when he knew it was time for mopping or picking up his garbage. The door would rush open, "Oh Lanie, I didn't know you were out here. (Yeah right!) Want to come in and have some coffee?" "No thanks." I would always reply. Then he would go on and on with offers until he would hopefully get me inside. I made the mistake of going into his apartment one time. It looked like, a very old bachelor apartment from the fifties. The slide projector was resting on a small dusty table just waiting for someone to press start. (Not today!)

As I started shoveling the snow, Andy came out telling me he would be happy to help me. After all shoveling snow was a man's job. I thanked him and told him it was part of my job and maybe he could help me another time with another job. (In your dreams) I finished shoveling the walk and paid a visit to our small but quaint local coffee shop around the corner.

The place was full. I saw the table I usually sat at had a gentleman sitting there. I decided to sit at the counter. A few minutes later he got up and came over to me. He said, "Excuse me I saw you were disappointed that I had taken your table." It was the only table for one.

"Oh, no, that's not my table, that's all right." And I went back to reading my script for my next acting class. He sat down next to me at the counter and introduced himself as Scott. I gave him my name and we got into a conversation. He seemed about in his mid-40's and well-dressed. No ring! I was pretty sure he wasn't from this neighborhood. He started asking me what I was doing in New York City. I told him I was an actress, dancer, and singer. He said to me, "I think I might be able to help you. Would you like to record a song with me?" Oh, boy, I thought.

"What did you have in mind?"

He told me he was a sometime record producer and continued to tell me something we might do together. "All I need for this recording session is another $90 for the musicians. If you can come up with the money, we may have a hit on our hands."

The song was *Wish Me a Rainbow*. It was the theme song for Natalie Woods' next movie. I would record the song then we could send out my recording to radio stations as a new single. If the movie hit, my song might hit!

Thinking back, I can't believe I said yes right away. But his story intrigued me. As my stepfather, George, once said, "You are a born sucker." I was now getting free rent, but that was helping me catch up. I didn't have a spare $90 to put into some possible record hit. Scott told me we had about a week to get the money together. I started thinking. I had my mother's jewelry, my grandmother's jewelry, and my aunt's jewelry. No one would miss it. My stepfather George might, if he knew I had sold my mom's antique jewelry on a $90 gamble. He wasn't crazy about my being an actress, but he loved me just the same. We had a very warm relationship. So I took the jewelry to a pawnshop on 42nd and Broadway. I walked in and said, "I need $90 for this." I lay the jewelry out on the counter. "Will this discover it?"

"Oh, sure, covers it perfectly." And he took out $90 in cash. (Notice my exquisite negotiating skills!)

"If you wish to get these items back," the owner explained, "bring me $90 the next time you have it." So I rationalized thinking they are not completely gone. I can get them back anytime. (Did I ever get them back? Don't ask.)

I recorded the song. They did play it on the radio — in the 6 AM timeslot. It was not exactly prime time, even so a fun experience. I recorded it as a professional in a real recording studio. I saw how engineers work behind the glass. I had a song on a 45 record to add to my resume. I also saved them money by being the children's voices we needed in the chorus. Was there anything I couldn't do? Talk about being full of myself!

The movie came out, the movie was a hit and the song was a hit — just not my version of it. Scott later informed me he wanted to be more than just my producer, no surprise there! As I was to learn in this, and future encounters with men, they all turn out to be married. (No ring? Yes, married!)

Once again, I came home to my solid gold apartment as the "super" for my building. I could now add, recording studio experience, to my resume.

CHAPTER 11

My TV Days

Auditioning for my *very first* soap opera was easily the most exciting moment so far in my new life. I had never been in front of a TV camera. When I arrived for the audition I was sent to a room where the actors and actresses rehearsed, before they go on camera. There were about12 girls, all looking like me, studying their "sides" (written dialogue from the part we were auditioning). There we were, all 12 of us, talking to ourselves, reading the lines of dialogue quietly out loud. We were going over them time and time again, trying different approaches to the character we hoped we would become. One by one our names were called. I watched each girl leave the room clutching our little script. The rest of us would smile and kind of merrily choke out, "Good luck!" Right, what we were really hoping for was maybe a stutter or a misread line — how about a freeze up! Just kidding —well maybe not! Even so, every one of us knew that the part had been written entirely for, "*me*!" And a little mess up from the competition would go a long way!

After seemingly hours of waiting for my name to be called (really 20 minutes!), I heard, "Miss Norton?" I rose to go through the door to the auditioning room that a young woman was holding for me. I was going to read opposite her for the audition. There was a long table in front of me filled with what looked like very important people. They had picked up my picture which was next in the pile of auditioning girls. There were whispers, looks that went around the table. "Whenever you're ready, Miss Norton," a man said. "You'll be reading with Janet our assistant. Take a seat, please." Janet was to read the part of my character's love interest. As we were reading, she never looked up once to offer any kind of emotional or physical interaction between us. I quickly understood that my job was to invent the appropriate response that my real lover might want from me. Monotone Janet was a new kind of reader for me. I am not criticizing her I know that was part of her job - reading flat so that I was the one who had to provide the performance.

Pardon me for interrupting my audition for a minute to emphasize how really passionate I had become about wanting to be an actress. Ever since I can remember, I practiced acting various emotions in front of my bathroom mirror. I remember I would feel a scene coming on at anytime day or night! I would run to the bathroom, which was next to my bedroom. I then began inventing and performing a scene in front of the mirror with my cast of characters, many times doing several different emotional interpretations of the same scene. This performing in front of a mirror was very fulfilling for me. I even accepted the academy award for best actress. (All wannabes do that!) I thanked all the important people and especially my mother of course. I started to cry as I finished my speech and bowed as I left the mirror. As you will soon see, it turned out to be extremely helpful in successfully managing my very first audition.

I particularly recall one of my bathroom scenes when I was in high school. I was standing in front of the mirror at my "mother's funeral!" I was grieving over her coffin. I started to cry. I was so stricken with sadness my crying led to sobbing. Apparently, I sobbed so loudly that my mother heard me. The next thing I knew she burst through the door to find me sobbing in front of the mirror.

"Lanie dear, what on earth is the matter? Why are you crying?" She put her arms around me.

"You just died!"

She plopped down on the toilet seat. "What in the world are you talking about?"

I couldn't help it. I started crying again. I looked at her face and cried really hard. "You looked so beautiful in that lovely blue dress just lying there peacefully in the coffin."

"Oh, Lanie, for heaven's sake, you and your acting will be the death of me!" Now I started really sobbing hard! "Oh now stop it you silly girl." We both hugged and laughed!

"I'm sorry, mom. When I get in a certain mood, I just have to practice in front of a mirror." I wiped my eyes and smiled broadly. "I'm getting really good at crying don't you think?"

"Yes dear. I can certainly vouch for that! Now please get me out of that coffin and you go do your homework. I could really use some peace and quiet around here." She muttered on her way out, "She will be the death of me!" as she shook her head from side to side.

"Okay, sorry mom," I called to her as I followed her out the door. (In my future TV career I was noted for crying on cue! See that, I wasn't crazy!)

So Janet and her totally unexpected flat-line reading did take me by surprise. Nonetheless, instead of panicking, I conjured up the scene in my head as I had done many times in front of the bathroom mirror. I began to feel more and more at ease. I felt I was really good! The more I read the more confidence I had. This would be my part, I was really feeling it. My *very first* audition and I was going to have....

"That's enough, Miss Norton!" broke midline into my reading. Then a very stretched out, "Thank you, — next please." The gentleman at the head of the long table had dismissed me!

I was completely devastated at the time — my very first audition! I rose and quietly left the audition room. But after 20 or 30, or however many times of, "Thank you, Miss Norton, next please." You learn to get up with grace and leave as if it were part of your routine. You just keep moving on to the next audition.

The next morning I found myself sitting on the couch wondering how I would be able to face the rest of the day. My very first audition and I had been dismissed midline. As I sat there torturing myself about my future in acting, my phone rang. No one really ever called me but my mother. And her call wasn't due for another hour. I answered the phone it was my agent Honey Raider, telling me I had a callback. I gasped, took a deep breath and managed, "You're kidding me!"

"No, I'm not. They want you to read on camera with the actor who will be your love interest." The pain from my curt dismissal faded instantly. I was going back to read live on camera, which I had never done before, with a real actor for a real TV soap opera. I couldn't believe it. I would be sent a set of lines to memorize for the call back. My agent interrupted my joyous moment by adding, "You do realize there will be a couple of other actresses on this callback. So learn those lines, girl, and give it everything you've got — this may be your big chance!" A quick little secret about the entertainment business, my agent probably had me and several other clients at the same preliminary audition and perhaps at this call back. She encouraged all of us with the same enthusiasm, worked hard for all of us, and never showed any partiality.

I can't go any further without praising my agent, Honey Raider! As I mentioned in my previous chapter, she has been, and currently is, my agent for my entire career. I had to call upon her many years later for some help. One of my 1972 commercials was being televised and I was not notified nor paid. I called Honey and told her the situation. She checked into it and found out they thought I was dead. Really! Big mistake. Huge! She persisted and negotiated a significant settlement for me. She received her 10% as she always did as my agent. Advertisers out there don't mess with Honey Raider's clients. Dead! What next?

I couldn't wait to get my lines. I wondered how many other girls would be doing callbacks with me. Soon after my lines arrived by bicycle delivery service, I felt so important, I spent the rest of the day memorizing them.

When I arrived the next day for my callback, there were only two other girls in the waiting room. We greeted each other cordially, wishing each other good luck. All of us seemed to look very different from each other. The direct was looking for a certain type but obviously was not sure what type that was. Someone magically had to be just what he was looking for. I hoped I would be that person. My callback experience was very different from my first audition.

The male actor was very helpful and encouraging as opposed to Janet's reading. Oddly, being on camera helped me rather than hindered me, I felt very comfortable in that spotlight. I remained that way throughout my career, lights, camera and action! No problem. Remember I had done two summer stock tours and been on stage in eight musicals all around the country. Add to that the shows love interest was tall and handsome. It was certainly easy to act as if I were in love with him.

We started the scene, quiet everyone — whenever you are ready.....
(It was a piece a cake!)

"Miss Norton, we will be making our decision promptly. Are you available to start next week?"

"Yes, I'm between jobs at the moment." This reaction to my audition gave me a lot of hope. But I knew I was not there yet. I spent the rest of the day and evening plaguing myself with doubts, should I have been more forceful here or more forgiving there? I'll bet I replayed that audition 100 times until I had to turn myself off from exhaustion. Actors do this all the time judging their performances, reading the lines again as if they were still auditioning.

The next morning I tried to distract myself by scurrying around the city doing what I do to maintain my existence. Every, I don't know, 15 minutes, half an hour I stopped at a phone booth to call my agent. "Did you hear anything yet?" "Patience dear," she would say. Another hour goes by, calling once more, "Did you hear anything yet?" I don't know what time of day it was, but this time, when I called Honey — she got on the line and said, "Well, Lanie dear, you did it, kid! (She always called me kid.) They loved you! They want you to start next week!" I could hardly breathe. I think I was jumping up and down like a cheerleader, twisting and turning! The person waiting patiently outside the booth had to know how ecstatic I was. The obvious excitement in my agent's voice told me that she was thrilled for both of us.

The soap opera was called, *"The Nurses."* This show was one of the last soaps to be filmed, wait for it — wait for it — to be filmed *live* in the studio! That meant when the director shouted action, we were live at that moment in everyone's living room in the "US of A!" LIVE! That's right, folks. My *first* time on TV was going to be *live!* Having more experience on stage than with live TV, I was especially nervous. The director I was going to be working with was famous for movies and TV and was from none other than Hollywood. At the dress rehearsal he stood real close to me brought his hands and fingers right up in front of my face in the shape of a square and said, "Lanie, this is the camera — that's all the audience is going to see of you!" He continued to explain that all the camera and audience would see is this much of my face. "This is not a stage so focus on your facial expression and don't make it too big. You are not playing to the balcony. Don't worry about your body movements." He was so nice to me.

We started to rehearse the scene I was in. With urgency in my step, I was to cross the floor from one side of the doctor's office to the other and then, delivered my line. Well, that didn't sound too difficult. (I only had one line. Did I forget to mention that?) With that being said and rehearsal completed, I went for wardrobe and makeup. There was a nurses costume waiting for me and once dressed I went for makeup, it was show time! "Live in 5," was heard over the loud speaker! Oh I thought, are we really going to do this? The director came over with some encouraging remarks. Keep it light, Lanie, keep it light. Relax. His words had the opposite reaction and I was frightened out of my mind! Another announcement was heard over the speaker. "Places please!" I stiffened up, almost paralyzed arriving at my spot just off the set. Then I heard the director shout, "Action!" Do you know how many times I heard, "Action" in front of my mirror?" Waking up from my panic attack, I saw the stage manager point to me and mouthed — go! Shocked back into reality, I found myself crossing to the other side of the doctor's office and stop. As I stood there waiting for the scene to finish, I can honestly say I don't remember saying my line. I remember crossing the floor in total fear and wonderment because millions — millions of people were watching! I was scared to death. I didn't remember having ever delivered that line. Then I heard Cut! Next scene please! I stood there blank. The other actors started to move toward me and whisper nice job, nice job. I smiled back, "Thanks. Thanks, it was fun." Liar, liar, pants on fire! I was terrified! My agent was the only person I told the truth to. She said I looked fine. Of course I had to ask her if I really delivered my line, she laughed, and said yes. I happen to be fortunate in the ability to memorize lines. My favorite spot was the bathtub! But for my first job, well, not a problem!

All that fuss for one line, multiple cameras, lighting, sound, makeup, blocking and who knows what else. I must have hyperventilated for hours afterward. There were no more live performances after that show. We followed the rest of the soaps and went to tape. No more cause for hyperventilating.

My character, Dorothy Warner, was a nurse who falls in love with a handsome orderly who would use her to help him steal drugs from the hospital. As you might imagine, my character was completely love-struck, incapable of refusing to help him. As the show progressed throughout the year, I finally was caught stealing and subsequently fired from the hospital. You guessed it, I was between jobs again! I learned quickly that in this business you find yourself often between jobs.

I learned a lot from my first TV soap opera. I learned that I lucked out going all the way from first audition to call back to signing a contract for the part. This is not the usual set of circumstances for actors in the business. Part of the dilemma for the actor is the need for an agent to get an audition. But you need to be working to get an agent. It's a catch 22 situation.

My luck started when an Equity company held an open-call for their summer stock tours. Anyone, with or without a union card, is permitted to audition for an open-call. I couldn't believe it, they hired me right on the spot! Since the company was an Equity company, I automatically got my Equity union card. Now an agent would see me to decide if they wanted to work for me. That's when Honey Raider came into the picture. I had another fortunate break when I got my TV soap opera job because then I also secured my Aftra card. (American Federation of Television and Radio) One more card left, Screen Actors Guild. This card is for television and movies. Bingo! I received that card also. *I* was very young to have all three union cards. Screen Actors Guild and AFTRA have since merged as one combined union. The merged unions are now called, SAG-AFTRA.

I also learned that being curtly dismissed in the middle of an audition does not always mean you lost the job. After you leave the room, you have no idea how you did. The people auditioning you rarely give any indication as to how well you performed. Sometimes during an audition, they can throw you a curve and may say, "Let's change it up a bit. Be a little more desperate when you're talking to him." That's possibly a good sign. They may be trying to see how well you take direction and can modify your performance.

My second soap opera, *Love of Life*, acquainted me with fans wanting autographs. As I walked out the stage door, there was a small group of people waiting almost at the doorway. A woman broke from the crowd holding a pad.

"Are you somebody?" She shouted waving her pen and pad in front of my nose. It was an autograph book.

"Well I don't know." I said, and laughed! "I'm leaving the studio after my first show on *Love of Life*. I'm a new character. Does that qualified?" I said.

"Wow, that's great! Congratulations! What's your name?"

"Leonie Norton."

"No, no," she said, "what's your character name?"

"Ah, yes of course! My character name is Kate Swanson." My first autograph seeker! No one had told me there would be people waiting outside the stage door after the show. I was trying my best to be fan-worthy. I had no idea about autograph protocol. Should I just sign my name? Should I write more than just my name? Should I use my regular name or my character name? Should I? Should I? Should I? She broke into my confusion with, "Well, uh, Kate Swanson. Will you sign my autograph book?"

"Yes, I would love to. Just so you know you are my first fan. How would you like me to sign it?"

The woman nervously handed me her autograph book and pen. "Make it to Julie Swick."

I took the book and signed my autograph, using my name not Kate's. I was barely finished when she snatched the book from my hands hurrying off to find someone else in the show to get their autograph in her book.

This was how I discovered my first TV soap opera fans. Each time we stepped out of the stage door, there they were waiting for us, loving us, asking us if you would take a picture with them. Could this autograph be for their grandmother, please? I was just delighted.

I had seen stars like the Beatles, the Supremes, the Beach Boys crowded around by fans in the news. Being the center of that kind of crowd was brand-new, very exciting and truly fun. I even received a few marriage proposals.

A few months later I was approached by a TV soap opera magazine. These magazines interview you and tell their readers about your life off-camera. You can look a little more into my past at: soapoperaworld. com and search Leonie Norton.

I would like to mention Julie Swick again (my first fan) because she followed me my whole career. She actually made me an afghan, a woolen blanket that she sent to the studio when I was on Love of Life. She sent me a Christmas gift made with love every year — even after I was no longer on TV, including last Christmas, always signing her letters "Your forever friend!" Thank you for that devotion Julie.

My character, Kate Swanson on, *Love of Life,* was once again in love, a secretary to a handsome boss who didn't give her the time of day. As with all people suffering with unrequited love, her heart is broken and her work suffers. The extreme stress trying to turn around her life leads to her drinking on the job. I remember my mother was very upset that I was playing a drunk on television. She fell right into believing it was real and wondered what the neighbors would think.

One day at Zabar's, a fancy delicatessen on Broadway and 73rd, I witnessed how seriously fans took our show. As I walked to the register to check out, I could see a woman bearing down on me with a nasty look in her eye. She confronted me and said, with some vigor, "Well, I see you have sobered up since noon! Honestly, you should be ashamed of yourself!" My jaw dropped. I started to say something, but she just kind of snorted, turned around, leaving my "shameful" person to consider my wayward life. I shouted something like it's only a TV show. She turned and shot me a disgusted look and bustled indignantly out of the store. I saw other people looking at me — what in the world is going on? Then I realized how much fun it was to be recognized in public. I started laughing. I rang up my bread, cheese and cold cuts, and left Zabar's wondering what my next confrontation with a fan would be like.

When I was on *Another World* my character was a nurse in love with a doctor. Often, when one of these fans discovers you in some public place, they cannot suppress their extreme excitement. I was shopping at Macy's. I had taken some dresses back to a changing room. I was in my bra and panties when the curtain was flung open! I tried to cover myself as best I could, kind of gasped, and said, "What's going on?"

An embarrassing face of a middle-aged woman was peeking around the edge of my dressing room curtain. She stammered trying to apologize. "Oh, my goodness, I'm so sorry Cindy! (Cindy was my character name.) I just couldn't help myself. I had to tell you, how wonderful you are and how I hope you and Russ get married! You make such a lovely couple. I'm so sorry to barge in like this. Please forgive me!" Just as quickly as she appeared — she was gone! I pulled the curtain back to reinstate my privacy. I was flattered, but I did undergo slight embarrassment being exposed like that. What we endure for the love of our fans!

Happily, I gained some peace of mind about my ability to make a living without having to sell doughnuts or clean toilets. My luck continued as another soap character was on my horizon. This realization and peace of mind slowly came as I moved from one show to another. I discovered that my fresh, cute, innocent look of the girl next-door was going to land me more and more work.

I have illustrated how difficult it is to get a TV soap opera job. Ironically, let me point out how unbelievably easy it is to be dismissed or written out as they say, from that job! When you sign on with a company, you have what is called a "one-way contract." This means, no way can *you* break the contract. At the same time you can be *fired* at any given moment. There are certain exceptions when an established, long running character wishes to leave for a movie or a vacation. They will be able to get permission and then return to their job. The writers simply write the character out for a while. I was never a permanent established character. I often had wished I were, but sooner or later it was bye-bye Lanie!

Here is my "one-way" contract experience that will interest you most. I was currently playing Cindy Clark on *Another World*. One of my fellow actors had taken a lengthy vacation abroad. I think it was for about a month. Upon returning he read in the script that he was going to be taking a lengthy tour to find his long-lost brothers. (Lengthy trips anywhere in these shows are not good!) He has just returned from a lengthy vacation. Now he comes home to find that he may face being written out of the show! In this business you learn quickly to read the handwriting on the wall. As you have probably guessed, he returned to discover that his lengthy tour to find his long-lost brothers could be forever!

He went to the producer to ask him if he were being written out of the show. The producer told him yes as the story was line was going in another direction. (Meaning, you are fired!) He asked the producer how long he had known about this? The producer responded, "Well, we didn't want to spoil your vacation. So we waited until now to let you know."

"Well thanks and no thanks! If I had known I was going to be fired, I wouldn't have gone on a vacation in the first place. I spent a lot of money in Europe, buying art and too much champagne!"

I commiserated with my friend when he told me his story. Thinking all the time how secure I felt about my job. I was going to marry Russ one of the main characters in the next couple of episodes. I was a really good nurse everyone loved Cindy Clark! I was Young. I certainly wasn't going to be written out. His character had been on forever! The television world was just waiting for our TV wedding!

I was in the fitting room, trying on my wedding dress. A gorgeous satin cream gown with lots and lots of lace!

"You like it?" asked the wardrobe lady.

"Love it, it's beautiful — but it seems to be a little too long. I'm sure you can take it up a bit."

The wardrobe lady looked at me with an unreadable expression — "Have you read the latest script, hon?"

"Not yet. I was just told to come in for a fitting."

"Well, my dear, you had better take a look at that script."

"And I should do that because? —"

"Because you are not, *walking* down the aisle!"

"Not walking? How do I go down the aisle then?"

"In a wheelchair!"

"In a wheelchair?"

"That's right, hon! Now, if I were you, I'd find out just what they have in mind for you. Get my drift?"

I had a sudden nauseous stomach! Unfortunately, I got her drift! Oh, no, could it be possible? Are they writing me out? As I was dressed and ready to leave, the wardrobe lady sidled up to me and whispered in my ear, "You didn't hear it from me, dearie, but I think you are dying of heart disease!" I felt like I might throw up. I was only 24, how could I die of heart disease at 24?

The next morning I walked into the producer's office and asked him the same question my fellow actor had asked. "Are you writing me out of the show?"

"Lanie, I'm sorry, yes we are. Russ has to be single again. He needs a new love interest. Our fans love him, and it's best if you die. Don't get me wrong. It has nothing to do with your performance. You have done a superb job for us. Remember, this is the soap opera business and — well, people love you as well, and it will be very sad if you die. Sad is great for the storyline also, and good for business.

There was an uncomfortable silence. He kind of fidgeted with a pen or something on his desk. I had to be sure I could walk before I stood up. I gathered myself, rose from my chair and put out my hand. We shook hands. I think I said something like, okay. My stomach was still nauseous.

I wasn't taking anything personally. Even though he was my boss, he had always been a friend. I had had a marvelous time performing on that show. Besides, he was right. The whole soap opera world cried at my wedding, and they cried at my death! People would stop me on the street holding back their tears, telling me how sorry they were that I had died. They would tell me they loved me. And they were so sorry Russ and I would never be together. They would go on and on! I would try to calm down their grief, but they were off before I could reach them.

I had always moved quickly from soap opera, to soap opera and was eager for my next audition. I knew I was still marketable as a love interest on other soaps. While waiting for my next soap, I got a call for my first commercial audition. I began to realize that my exposure on soaps, would lead to TV commercials. Ban deodorant, Sherman Williams paints, AT&T and many, many more. I was famous for the Wisk, ring around the collar commercial — "Oh, those dirty rings!" (If you would like to view the spot: youtu.be/ifXop1d7ntU). As a matter of fact people would stop me on the street, look at me, sometimes put their hands on their hips, and say, "Oh, those dirty rings!" Other times people would pass me singing, "Ring around the collar, ring around the collar." And I would laugh with them as they waved to me.

One of my favorite times shooting a commercial was singing for the deodorant product called, Shower To Shower! "A sprinkle a day keeps the odor away, have you had your sprinkle today?" I was singing in a shower wearing a two piece bathing suit only my shoulders and head were seen. Such fun!

Even though doing commercials was good money, I did one commercial that… well, you'll see! The product was an antacid. I had no lines. I was at a diner sitting on a counter stool with 4 other actors, eating huge, greasy hamburgers. Unfortunately, there were many "takes" (meaning, times they had to shoot trying to get it right!). They would start the scene and simultaneously we would start eating our burgers. Before I was finished eating, I would hear the director shout, "Cut!" At this point I would spit out my large chewed bite of hamburger into the-soon-to-be-disgusting "spit bucket." They put it on the floor next to our counter stools. This bucket was large and designed especially to collect food for these types of commercials. So think about 30 takes eating and swallowing all that food. Good heavens, besides gaining a lot of weight, I probably would have been sick by the end of the day. So that's the good news about having a "spit bucket". The bad news is how gross it became during this particular shoot. In this commercial, the director was looking for a face that expressed especially painful heartburn.

"Cut! Let's try it again……. and — Action!"

A camera films from all different angles so there were many takes. Sometimes there is a lighting problem or sound problem. I continued eating and burping and spitting, eating, burping and spitting!

I don't remember how many takes there were, but I knew I had to do something to get it right. I remembered a specific day when my mother took a bite of something, then made this awful face and burped. She told me it was her heartburn. It was kind of a gasp, but inward, a very weird twisted look on her face and eyebrows. Then my poor mother let air blow out followed by an amazing burp. I decided to try to re-create my mother's reaction to heartburn. (Sorry mom!)

The camera came in for a close-up. I was ready. "Quite please — Action!" I took a huge bite of my hamburger, chewed a bit, then gave my all to what I thought was a look of intense heartburn. I twisted my eyebrows and face as hard as I could, took a deep breath inward, followed by letting air out the side of my screwed up mouth, ending with a loud burp. To my great relief, the next thing I heard was that phrase always extremely welcome from the director "Cut!" — "That's a wrap!" I spit out my last bite of the huge greasy hamburger into that gross and disgusting bucket! I gathered my thing and met a friend waiting for me who suggested we go celebrate my getting a commercial. I answered, "Thank you. Great idea! Where should we go?" My friend said, "How about Steve's Burger Bar?" (No comment!)

When I saw the commercial on TV, guess whose face appeared giving out one large burp, for all America to see? Thanks mom, you did a great job!

My Ban Deodorant commercial turned out to be somewhat embarrassing. I was sitting on the couch with two young children. It was an all-American Saturday night — parents out, babysitter with children. The scene was cliché calm and peaceful with children falling asleep, babysitter watching TV. Suddenly a voice-over shatters the ambience —"It's 10:00 on Saturday night! What are *you* doing?" In response I lift my arm, turn my head, and cautiously smell my armpit. I turn my head back to the camera, wrinkling my forehead, and in open-mouthed horror, displaying the discovery of an unpleasant odor wafting from my armpit! Thank goodness, no one ever smelled their armpit as they passed me on the streets of New York!

Sometimes I would land a commercial that took me out of town or, "on location" as was the term. I was flown first class, stayed at a nice hotel with per diem for food and expenses. I felt a little bit like the winner on Queen for a Day. At the time you want this heavenly job never to end. You kind of feel like you're walking on air from one of these commercials to another, with no end in sight, but...

Later in my career I was at a party with a group of actors. We had auditioned together and became friends. There was an older quiet woman there who wasn't getting the attention that I was. She caught my eye. Being younger and early in my career, she said to me, "I was where you are right now. I remember thinking this will never end." She shook her head and continued, "Enjoy it now because it does end. One day, you are not that young all-American girl next-door anymore. Your callbacks will become fewer and fewer."

Wow! Talk about dead silence as a cold wind blew through me! I remember feeling that I had the breath knocked right out of me. I said nothing trying to get it back. At the time, I believed this would never happen to me. I was a successful soap opera star. I would always be working. Need I say you know what's coming of course it happened to me. It happens to all of us because there is always someone younger, more eager, more beautiful just waiting in the wings to take that job that used to be yours.

However, at that particular point, my time had not yet come. I did commercials for many more years. Made lots of money, but as I mentioned, I always remembered what she said and the sad, wistful look on her face. When my time did come, I fortunately learned how to reinvent myself. Apparently, this particular former actress did not have that ability.

I had special pleasure in watching some people I had worked with go on to become very famous in the movies. When I was on *One Life to Live* I was married to, Tommy Lee Jones. Tom Berenger played my brother. Hugh Marlowe was the doctor. Hugh was a big movie star in the 50's. I loved working with Rue McClanahan from, The Golden Girls. She played my mother on *Another World*.

As that woman had forecast for me that I would begin losing footholds in TV soap operas and commercials, I am proud to say my TV soaps and commercials career took me to age 45. You will discover in another chapter that I was undaunted in discovering other ways to perform. You can't keep a good actress from hunting down her next job.

And my father said I was worthless. Well look at me now dad. Would you believe he never once commented on my career? I learned early in my life, not to wait for other people's approvable or praise. My mother, god bless her, would still have preferred I marry Steve, the pharmacist. Go figure!

However, after age 45 I did a couple of stutter steps backward and had a small part on a TV show called *Las Vegas*. I was to play the part of a Midwestern mother who had just found out her son was dead. That son had left a baby boy. I was seeing the baby for the first time in my scene. I was handed my son's baby, I acted extremely happy. Over the loudspeaker the director said, "Cut! Remember your son is dead. Don't overdo the happiness." "Sorry! Okay, I got it." One more time and we got it. I had no lines but I didn't care, I loved it. The sweet smell of the makeup room, the wardrobe, the lights, camera, and ....

The only other appearance I had on a prime time TV network was to play a hooker. Yes, hooker! My agent called — last-minute audition at 4 o'clock today! "You're going to be a hooker!" That gave me 45 minutes! Honey continued, "Put on whatever you think a hooker might wear and get yourself over to that audition pronto!"

"What's the address?" She rattled off an address in downtown Manhattan. I could make it, but I had to take a cab. Right at rush hour! Getting a cab at rush hour... Don't ask!

My big chance to be on a nighttime TV network series, but a hooker! Mom is really going to love this. I was the all American girl. I know I had also been a drunk at one time. I don't even drink! I had a brief conversation with myself and came up with this result. I'm an actress, if they want a serial killer, I could act like a serial killer. What am I worried about? My job is acting. Get some appropriate clothes on, Lanie, and get out there, get to that audition. A nighttime TV network series — go get it, girl!

I put on as revealing a top as I could find. I found a short black skirt to put over my stockings and garter belt. The 6 inch spike heels on my red shoes were killing me. I teased my hair up, smeared on a ton of makeup, and slapped on the gaudiest jewelry I could find. I got this I thought. I'm standing on Broadway and 79th, chewing gum vigorously, waving my arms frantically and gyrating my hips. I got a cab so fast I couldn't believe it! They almost had an accident rushing to be the first to pick me up. I stepped into the closest cab and took on my character — never too early to be the part!

The driver turns round, looks me up and down says, "Where to, babe? You're lookin' real good, mama!"

"Thanks, doll." I don't think I had ever called a male *doll* in my life! "Take me to 44th and Fifth Avenue and step on it! I gotta be there in 15!"

"I'll just bet you do, sweetheart. Hold on!" He hit the gas. We were off. I had to hold onto the handle at the top of the window as he was definitely a veteran New York City cabbie. Stop, start, around this car, beep at that car — your life is in their hands. I never had an accident in a cab in the city. I don't know if I'm proud of that or not?

"You are a cutie," I said. I may as well practice for the audition right now. I had the perfect situation.

"No, kiddin'?" He kept turning around looking at me meanwhile driving like a maniac.

"You bet, doll. You're just my type. But you have to keep your eyeballs on the road, honey. I see you checking me out in your rearview. I don't want to arrive at my appointment DOA!"

He laughed. "Not this hombre. I ain't been in a wreck oh, maybe six months. Say, how about this. You and me, hook up about 5 o'clock when I'm off the clock! Waddaya say?"

Am I really going to do this? So out of my mouth comes, "Sure doll, what are ya thinkin' of? How much money ya got? The more you want the more it's gonna cost ya. You know that doll you been around the block."

"My tip box is overflowing. I'd sure like to find a way for you to get it baby, catch my drift, sweetheart?"

"I sure do, honey!" I was trying to stay in character wondering how far I was going to go! Once again out of my mouth comes,

"Well, doll, how about this! I am gonna meet you, uptown corner of 90th and Columbus, five on the dot! How's that." We were almost to my destination.

"You're on, mama! Man, did I luck out picking you up!"

"Thanks, baby!" He pulls up to my building. I climb out of the cab, searching for what I owe the guy, including a big tip.

"Baby, you made my day! You sure are somethin'!" I stick my hand with the money in it through the window. He pushes my hand back. "Gorgeous, let's just say this ride is on the house, because I know how good you gonna treat me tonight!"

Now I'm embarrassed. "Oh, no, that's all right Doll! You make your living your way, and I make my living my way. It's yours, hombre, you got me here on time – and alive!" We both laughed.

"You're all right, sweetheart. Okay. Wow, heavy tipper too! You're the best, mama."

I gave him a wink through the window and said, "See you at five, honey lamb!" I turned and did my best hooker walk toward the entrance of the building.

I created a little chatter and a lot of looks as I found my way to the audition room. When 5 o'clock rolled around, I did wonder how long the poor guy waited for me. I felt a little bad. But I did give him a good tip. Ah, life in the City!

There was another actress waiting when I arrived at the audition. She just looked normal. We were both asked to come in together. That was unusual. I was still in character. I also had a large blue bag full of possible hooker clothing with me.

The director said, "So, what have we got here girls?"

I answered first staying in character, "If you're not happy with what I got on, honey lamb," (I stood modeling my hooker clothes) "I do have a lot of other fun stuff that I could wear." I opened my bag and began to display my other possible hooker clothing. See anything ya like?

"Oh, that's wonderful! I already love what you have on."

"I made all this stuff myself."

"Really," he gave me a long approving look.

He turned to my competition. "What about you?"

"I don't really have anything."

Not missing a beat, standing with my hands on my hips, "So what does that make me — a slut?"

We all laughed.

You guessed it, I got the part! Lesson one for all you would be actresses/actors. Don't ever be in a position where you tell the director, "I don't have anything!" Lesson two, you are an actress and there's no part that you can't take — and kill it!

I was well aware, that someday I might not be on TV soaps or commercials, but I was determined to continue working in the entertainment business. I simply had to find a new way to express myself. I love performing, and making money is not too bad either.

From hooker to clown! After my last TV spot, I jumped on the band wagon going to cable TV. That's right, cable TV was just starting out and a friend of mine suggested we put my clown show on cable. You will read about the transformation and reinvention of Lanie into a clown, in chapter 14, My Life After 45.

The above picture, is Sparkles the Clown, from "Birthday Parties Are Us," a cable TV.

I don't think that "cab driver" would meet *me* on 92nd street! Then again.......?

CHAPTER 12
An Actress has a Baby

I was 29 when my daughter Samantha was born. *One Life to Live* had an actress who wanted to leave the show. The producer wanted me to play her character. He talked to the actress who wanted to leave about staying until I could replace her. I told the producers it would just be a few days until I could come to work. The actress agreed to stay until I was ready. Every few days the show would call my agent. Is Lanie ready yet? Seven days after I gave birth, I showed up for work. Everyone tells you how your life will change dramatically when you have a child. Forget 9-to-5, Monday through Friday, you now have a job 24/7 for the rest of your life! More than that, you will discover you will, *never not* be a mom! (My mom, in the picture top left.)

Returning to my Soap Opera life brought with it a whole set of new issues. One of my immediate problems, since I was breast-feeding, I had to watch I did not leak onto my blouse while on camera. I was never sure what was going to stimulate my milk to rise to the surface looking for my baby! A sanitary napkin stuffed in my bra worked quite well to ward off the leakage. Brand-new mothers also suffer constant flatulence. This was so funny and so embarrassing. I would kind of putt-putt my way from one scene to another. Putt, putt, putt across the studio floor hoping no one would hear me — knowing everyone did! Even though I had reached the age of 30, I could not prevent my face from flushing when my (call it like it is!) *farting* propelled me from one set to the other.

Dilemma number two, needing to express my breast milk, a couple of times during a day's taping. My understanding producers gave me a small refrigerator for my dressing room. There I would express my milk, bottle it, put it into the refrigerator. After almost a year of this routine, I decided to switch to bottle feeding.

During that first week of shooting, I discovered makeup artists are indispensable and among the unsung heroes. You've seen enough TV and movies to know that woman must push extremely hard as the baby begins to emerge from her body. I was one of those women who pushed so hard for so long I had broken blood vessels all over my face, which were still visible as I went back to work a week later. The makeup artist looked at me, smiled with great confidence, and told me she would take care of that for me. "When I'm finished, honey, no one will know the difference."

Thank you my angel. You were right. It was impossible to distinguish any marks on my face. I felt relaxed, ready to be on camera.

All new mothers know how anxious you are to leave your new baby with someone else even for a short time, even if it's a close relative. I had a friendly relationship with my wardrobe lady who solved this problem. She had three grown children and offered to take care of my baby whenever I needed her. My instincts told me that she would be gentle and protective with my little treasure. My general rule was I would try to do my extra activities when she was available. I wanted to be with my new baby daughter as much as possible. Unfortunately, I was not able to bring her on set. Once she got older, about 5, I brought her with me on many commercial auditions. I was blessed with a wonderful child who adjusted to my career activities. Sometimes there was an actor friend of mine up for the same part who offered to watch her during my audition. Other times, bless her little heart, she would sit quietly on a chair or on the floor with her stuffed animal or a book.

On one occasion I had a two week job in upstate New York. That particular time I left her with her father. I was very unhappy to be away from her. I could never get home fast enough from a job. I would rush through the door, not even take off my coat. I just had to hold her in my arms and kiss her over and over until she started laughing! The upshot was, I made a rule, I would turn down any job outside New York City. That left out theatre jobs in the surrounding states. I may have lost some key contacts, but my heart was at peace, and my baby was loved. Another rule I stood by was never taking a job longer than one maybe two nights. But I didn't care, I loved being with my Samantha. She was so much fun to be with. I originally thought it was only going to be hard in the early years. I was soon to find out it was always going to be challenging. But I was determined to be there for her.

Hopefully each generation will learn from the last and make family life better and better. I know that has happened in Sam's family. Samantha is the joy and love of my life. She has grown up to be an incredibly strong and intelligent woman. I hope you don't mind, I'm going to be immodest and include a poem my daughter wrote for me on my 60th birthday. My heart swelled reading this poem.

MY MOM
By Samantha Koppelman

Who she is, would not be described by clothing by height or by hair
color - nor by the car she drives or the company she keeps
My mom is a vision
She appears, she excites, she plays
You feel a glowing warmth touch your heart, the inner part of you,
when you know her that is - only, when you truly know her
She can change a child's world like no other
She speaks to animals and to those who have passed on
Her spirit is a rainbow that can hold everything and everyone she
loves, inside her
There is always room for you in my Mom's world
She gives, She loves
She is pure
She is so, so very beautiful
My Mom is as actress
My Mom is a clown, a teacher, a poet, a friend, an artist, a dancer,
a singer, a lady
My Mom is a Do—er, She makes things happen
She is a healer
My Mom smells like a sunny day in the park, that sometimes takes
me back to age six
My mom hugs through you, you can always feel her
My Mom makes believe all the time
She can be, see and create anything she wants
My Mom tells Apple juices stories and my Mom rubs my head
My Mom loves and laughs – she simply lives......oh so simply, she lives
My Mom is my heart, my joy and my greatest friend

Leonie "Lanie" Norton
and Jim Norton

The Koppelman family — Samantha, husband Sean and son, Max — and, *my* family too.

Samantha and her husband Sean have given me an amazing grandchild, Max Koppelman. Watch out everyone, I see wonderful things for all of us in his future. I am very envious of Max having Sean as a father. Sharing my family history, I have told Sean many times, I wish he had been my father. For the first time in my life I got to see how a loving father and mother treat their child. I saw all the things I missed, the fun, love, laughs, hugs and kisses and most importantly, communication. Samantha's family has been a very important part of my life. To watch my daughter and her husband love my grandson, has sometimes brought tears to my eyes. I have never seen such loving, caring parents in my life. I sometimes wonder what my life would have been like if they had been my parents. They are in my life now and that's all that matters.

Aside from being the greatest parents, they also work together in their own company, The Talent Magnet, a boutique search firm in NYC.

I have been truly blessed. Thanks you for always being there for me. The older I get the more it is appreciated.

CHAPTER 13

Life on the Underside of New York City

Is living in New York City amazing? Definitely! Is living in New York scary? Sometimes! Would I trade my 40 some years living in the heart of Manhattan for anything? Not on your life! My early days in the city showed you how fun exciting and amazing part of my life was. Now I'm going to tell you about, the not so fun part of my life living in New York City.

You're probably reading this sometime in the year 2020. If you are from NYC, I am confident you have learned to lock your car, lock up your bike, your umbrella, etc. If you are female, you don't walk anywhere alone in the dark in any neighborhood.

Remember I was a poor struggling actress when I started living there. I rode a bicycle. In terms of time it was better than an automobile. I would race in and out of traffic, slip over on sidewalks when I had to go to auditions easily on time. Yes, I had my lock and chain always with me and always locked up my bike. Remember, this is a rough town. One time I emerged from an interview and my bike was no longer chained to the pole. I soon discovered that a bicycle was not safe chained any longer. The same cutters that you use to cut through a chain-link fence will obviously cut through any bicycle lock. Maybe this is a business for some people. They drive around the city with their large bolt cutter stealing bicycles. Then sell the stolen bikes! The police were of little help in this case, because you're in New York City. In 1980 the population was 7 million plus! They had bigger things on their mind. I was then brought back to subways, buses, and my trusty feet.

I inherited my mother's automobile after she died. My mom was always there for me, even after death. The car had a minuscule trunk that was surrounded by windows, so everything in the car was exposed. I would have to be very careful and not leave anything in the car I didn't want stolen. I was truly grateful because there was no more schlepping up and down subway stairs, or lifting up my cart onto a bus. Of course, I did have the added issue of parking if I was not in a suburb type neighborhood.

Parking in NYC-101 entailed which side of the street you could park on, for that particular day at that particular time, and for what length of time. Then there were the cars from New Jersey and Long Island that came in every day taking up spaces causing me to go around and around the block until a space opened up. Then I had the joy of using my skilled parallel parking which all of us are born with (yes I'm being sarcastic!).

The result of failing one of the tests in, *Parking in NYC-101* was getting an expensive fine. You were on the wrong side of the street after all. This was not a day you can even park on this street. Yes, you were parked correctly, but your meter ran out, or the final blow, having your car towed! I will not take the time to tell you the impossible contortions you must endure to find out where your car has been towed!

When you do find out where your car is, will you have enough money to get your car out of the police lot? Probably not. When that happened to me, I must thank my stepfather, George, for lending me the money. After which he thankfully said no need to pay him back and hugged me. He was always there for me when I needed him. Thanks George!

Another surprise encounter with my car in NYC goes something like this. I wake up one morning and go down to my car, that is if I can remember where I parked. I then look for certain things. Is it still there? Yes. Is there a ticket on the windshield? No. Has it been broken into? No. There is a tremendous sigh of relieve. A warm glow of happiness fills my heart. Another success story to tell the neighbors! I can now safely focus on my destination.

I had planned on visiting my friend who was in the hospital. When I arrived, I found a parking space just outside the hospital and legal too! It was broad daylight, no need to be concerned about safety! Going over *Parking in NYY-101,* daytime in front of the hospital with lots of people coming and going, should be safe. But, in New York City, people only look straight ahead they probably know that's for their own good. Don't misunderstand me. We do have our everyday heroes. They just aren't around…., everyday.

My friend and I visited for just about 45 minutes. I wished her well and turn to exit. Returning to my car there is no thought in my mind for my cars safety. Everything was, "copacetic." Wrong answer! As I get closer — Oh, no! My car has been broken into! How did they get in? Why did they get in? My mom's cheap old tiny car, which has only one speaker, no high fidelity nor any 120 decibel woofer, (like I know what that is) has been ransacked! What could they possibly have wanted or thought they could steal and sell? First I see the windshield wipers are missing, then I noticed that the back left rear window is gone! I mean, really? Who wants one rear window for resale?

I was standing looking at my car with everything scattered all over as if they had been told there was gold inside. Before that time I had never experienced the feeling you get when you're private property is invaded by a stranger. I had a sick feeling in the pit of my stomach. As I stood there feeling violated, I thought thank god I didn't have my clown show paraphernalia inside. Now that would have been a real disaster. So much for *Parking in NYC-101*!

When I moved to Brooklyn I thought Samantha and I would be safer there. Her father and I had divorced and I needed a place for us to live.

Remember I mentioned what a disaster it would be if I had left my clown show in the car that was broken into? Really, I was only gone for a brief moment. And that's all it took to clean me out of my keyboard, magic bag, puppets, etc. I guess we have to say, Brooklyn life — was not safer, but hopefully not as expensive. Wrong about that too!

We also fell prey to a local car thief business. My daughter and I had rented some movies. I was going to the car to return them to the video store. Wait a minute — where's my car? Oh, no problem. Guess I forgot I left it on the other block. I went to the other block — still no car! My confusion veered toward reality and — you guessed it — my car had been stolen! I reported it missing. Unlike my stolen bicycle, it took the police only two days to find it.

I was told my car was at a local Brooklyn collision repair center. When I arrived at the garage, a man handed me an estimate of what it was going to cost me to put my car back in shape. I told the man I already had a company that I dealt with and my guy would pick up the car sometime that day. Thanks anyway.

I could see as I was explaining he was not happy at all because he kept shoving the estimate in my face. His face was getting redder by the moment. I didn't know what was going on. I didn't like the guy or his aggressive behavior. What was his problem? I quickly thanked him again and got out of there. My guy did pick the car up later that day.

I found out from a friend of mind in Brooklyn just what happened to me and why the garage owner was so angry. Apparently the police have a list of collision repair centers. When a car is stolen they call the garage on the *top* of the list to tow the car to their repair shop. The police try to be fair and give each repair center a turn to retrieve the stolen car for repairs. Their name then goes on the *bottom* of the list. This particular garage was next on the list. The owner had his workers steal a car so that they would get the towing job faster and make the money. So when I wouldn't let him repair my car, he became angry — now his garage was at the bottom of the list! Obviously, patience was not his virtue.

I don't know if I was lucky or not, but my car was never again stolen. I guess living in Brooklyn wasn't as safe as I though. You just can't make this stuff up. To this day I still have dreams about losing my car. I'm in New York wandering the streets in search of my vehicle. Or worse, find my vehicle with smashed windows and slashed tires having no way to get home. It's better than being on stage and forgetting my lines! That's a nightmare!

It's not only my car that has been accosted in New York City, I am among New Yorkers who have been accosted mugged — and more than once! New Yorkers use the word mugged to mean you are stopped in the street, you are asked for your valuables, you comply — the two parties then go their separate ways. You don't report a mugging unless you are a tourist.

This particular time I had spent a week with my friend Bonnie, one of the 73st girls, at her home in Chicago. My mom had recently passed and she invited me to rest and take time to heal. I was on my way home. At the time I was living with three new girls since the other three 73rd street roommates had gone on to new adventures. In the entertainment business, people are always coming and going. When one person leaves, you find someone else to come in to pick up that part of the rent. We each had a key to get into the building and a key to get in our apartment on the fourth floor. My cab from the airport dropped me off. I entered my building and waited for the elevator. The door opened I stepped in and pressed #4. The elevator stopped and opened on the third floor. A well-dressed young man entered carrying a folded newspaper in his hand. In a matter of seconds he pulled a knife out from between the newspaper he had been carrying and put it to my throat — so I could feel the blade! "Shut the fuck up! Shut the fuck up! Shut the fuck up!" I hadn't said a word. I froze! I stared at the floor — another New York rule — if the mugger sees your face, he might be motivated to now kill you because you may be able to "finger him" out of police mug shots!

"Give me all your money!"

"I don't have any — honestly! I just came from the airport."

"Don't give me that shit! You have money! Now give it to me!" He was shouting — I was staring at his shoes. I was so frighten I couldn't think, then all of a sudden —

"Wait a minute, wait a minute! I do have some money. I just remembered."

"Yeah, yeah, hand it over — now!"

Frantically I searched in my purse to find I had $60 left from the weekend with Bonnie. Shaking all over, hyperventilating, maintaining my view of the floor, I pushed the money up to him. He grabbed it with a snarl! The knife blade had cut me — I could feel I was bleeding slightly. My hand went to my neck, my eyes darted to his face then just as quickly back to the floor. Oh my god! I made the one mistake you never ever make, I looked at his face. Oh no! Now he's going to slit my throat — I really believed it. I felt faint. I could hardly breathe.

The elevator stopped — he must have pushed a button when he saw the money coming out of my purse. He shot out of the elevator pushing the button for the top floor so he could make his getaway down the stairs. I had never been so shaken and felt so close to death! When I got to my floor, I stumbled out of the elevator. I felt my throat and saw blood on my hand. I rushed to my apartment. None of my roomies were home! Of all the times to be alone! I called the police. They showed up about 20 minutes later to get my statement and show me some mug shots. At that point I could not have recognized my mother! I was so out of sorts! They flipped through photos for me. I pretended to try to focus on a possible recognition of my mugger.

Finally, I said I'm sorry I really don't recognize any of these men. I didn't get that good of a look at him. I spent most of the time looking at his shoes. I wasn't very brave. "You did the right thing, miss. You could be dead right now!" That was comforting. I took their card and said goodbye to the officers. I assessed my financial situation. I was now out $60 of my rent money for the month. I was in a children's musical as Cinderella and made $25 a show, giving four shows a week. Rather meager I know.

But it was money, it was acting and it could be part of my resume — so I worked it.

Fast forward to me living in a brownstone apartment building on west 81st in Manhattan, I am now 48 years old running my own children's entertainment business. The place is called "The Chuckles Fun House." I gave children's birthday parties which included a clown show with magic, music, face painting, puppet show, lunch and cake. Each birthday person got a video of their party. The apartment was on the first floor with stairs leading up to the front door. The building was attached to a large nursing facility with lots of people coming and going. Even though I was on the first floor, I felt very safe. Many of the workers from the facility would sit on the steps of my building when taking a break, their presence made me feel doubly safe. Did I mention there was a small window that over-looked the little court yard next to the set of steps? It had a small air conditioner that fit in the left side of that window. The right side had an expandable fan that closed up the rest of the window. For all intents and purposes it was a safe place to live. After all, it was not on street level.

My apartment had a large flowing dining room adjacent to a small kitchen then a spacious living room. I slept in a tiny room in the back. Both large rooms had huge ornate marble fire places. It was quite a grand place, perfect for parties. I set the rooms up accordingly. That tiny room reminded me of my first apartment on 19th street. I lived at this apartment by myself on weekends when I did parties. I was married to my second husband at the time and he was living with his son, Kyle, in New Jersey.

New York City is never totally quiet — any time of day or night. This night was a normal night. It was no different whether you were 19 or 90 you recognized the sounds that made you feel safe. I had felt safe for many months living next to the nursing home. Many of the workers were my friends.

"Having any parties this weekend, Miss Clown?"

"You bet George!" They were always looking for leftover birthday cake.

That night as I slept in my tiny dark room I was awakened by an *unfamiliar* sound. Not loud or easily recognizable, but it was there. I sat up in bed to listen more intently — no further sound. But I knew I had heard something. Should I check it out? I continued to stare at the tiny door to my tiny room. It was closed. I heard the sound again. I was now certain I heard an unfamiliar sound coming from behind my bedroom door. Good lord, the doorknob was turning! The door eased open revealing a short, dark, full figure of a man in my doorway — his ghost-like figure looming as I saw the glint of a knife blade. The rasping sound of his quick breaths turned my stomach. He stood five feet from my bed. What now? In a flash he was on me. I was on my bed struggling with a strange man, a knife at my throat! As we struggled I finally screamed, "I have no money! I have no money!"

He immediately stopped, sat up, and let me go. We both sat on the edge of the bed for a moment — both of us breathing hard. My whole body shuddering. My brain kicked in. "Wait a minute — Wait a minute. I do have money." I reached down, grabbing my purse. He stayed still watching me — his hand with the knife no longer at my throat.

Ruffling through my purse, I remembered I had $80. "Here!" He grabbed the money. I tried to keep my face from looking at his and said,

"Are you going to rape me?" (How in the world that came out of my mouth, I'll never know.)

I chanced to glance at his face as he displayed a disgusted look — dropped his head low and shook it from side to side, and said,

"I'm not that kind of robber."

He then got up grabbed the phone and cut the wire. "Don't move for 10 minutes!" My face was still looking down when I heard his footsteps leaving the room. When I had the courage to look up, he was gone. I was frozen in time.

Gradually, I felt sensation returning to my body. I rushed upstairs to my neighbor's apartment. I had no idea what time it was. I banged on their door, "Janis, Harry! It's me, Lanie, from downstairs. I've been robbed!" A few moments later the couple opened the door in their bathrobes.

"Lanie, oh you poor dear, tell us what happened? Come in, come in, sit down." I was still shaken and in shock. They called the police while I went to their bathroom to assess the damage. They said they saw blood on my neck. I peered at myself in the mirror. The mirror looked back at me in my pink nightgown and my terrified eyes. I was trembling and bleeding slightly from the neck. I was attempting to comprehend the reality of moments ago — of having been struggling with a strange man with a knife at my throat on my bed in my bedroom! That was the closest to being raped and murdered in my life!

Keeping with tradition in New York City, the police arrived with a book of mug shots extremely familiar to the one they had shown me 20 years ago. I gave them the same answer I had given them 20 years ago. Sorry, I really didn't see his face it was so dark. And I was so frightened! I took their card, once again, and they left.

My neighbors let me use their phone to call my husband. He jumped in his car and drove all the way from Jersey to be with me. My husband stood guard the rest of the night. We went home to New Jersey the next day.

I didn't return to the city for three weeks. That's how long it took me to be able to sleep alone successfully. Upon my return, my husband accompanied me and securely boarded up the half a window that held the extended screen which had also been the entrance for my intruder. He used screws instead of nails.

Did I relive this experience many more times in my life — no comment.

It was the scariest moment of my life. At the time, did I really believe my life was in danger? No. I was too frightened to think. Am I lucky to be telling this story? Yes. The real question is — would I change anything about my life in New York City? Not on your life. (Or mine!)

CHAPTER 14
Life After 45

I forgot I would eventually be forty some years old. Where am I now? Screeching around corners in my subway seat underground in New York City, heading for 34th and Broadway — dejected! You might notice I was not in a taxi learning my lines for my latest soap opera job or preparing for a commercial. Unbelieving, I hearkened back to that older actress who, that day in my house had prophesied exactly what she believed to be my future — I was heading for my first 9-to-5 office job! I had gotten older. Young people did start coming up in the ranks in both soap operas and TV commercials. I had lost my marketability! Or perhaps I was not aggressive enough! If they wanted me to take jobs out of town, I still remained firm in my position to not leave my daughter. I loved this time with her. I was divorced and that presented problems.

In this office job I was hired to do filing. No, filing was not on my resume, but here I was. I couldn't remember ever being in "an office" — a monster space with cubicle after cubicle after cubicle — office manager's job was behind glass at the rear of the office. This corporate creature was void of any personality. Pretty much everything was "real estate beige." The water cooler was the most exciting item in the room. Light years away from the hustle and bustle of excitement, lines being rehearsed, costumes,

makeup, autographs and dressing rooms. Being noticed! Lest we forget
— "Quiet on the set everyone, camera and — Action!"

I was making $7 an hour — believe it or not, this was a good pay in
1983 the minimum wage was $3.35.

I'm sure you remember singing the alphabet song when you were in
elementary school — that was filing but on a higher level! In the cubicle
next to me was Ginny. Ginny was in her 60s, little overweight, banal glass
frames, and, poor soul, starting to show thinning hair. After the fourth day
on the job I saw my neighbor Ginny with these little rubbery things on
her fingers — they look like little hats. Ginny and I had a neighborly relationship — not lunch together yet, pretty much she brought hers anyway,
but we said hello every morning and had some small talk at the water
cooler once in a while. I decided to ask her about the little rubbery hats.

"Oh, these little things." She held up her hands wiggling her little hats.

"Yes, what are they for?"

"Well, Lanie, when you've been around here as long as I have, you'll
probably have to be wearing these too. Your finger tips will be so smooth
that it will be difficult for you to slip through the papers and will take twice
the time to file. Time is money you know, and wasting time is frowned
upon in the corporate world."

I looked into her pleasant expression and asked, "Ginny, how long
have you been working here?"

She proudly announced, "30 years, yep, 30 years, quite a while."

THIRTY years? Singing the ABC song with little rubber hats on my
fingers? 30 years! How about SEVEN days! Seven days and I was out of there!

After hearing Ginny, on my 30 minute subway ride home I knew I
had to get serious about my future. I have to admit I was scared. I really
didn't want to work in an office. I am an actress. So this was the first of
many times I would have to reinvent myself and fast. We had gone through
my money pretty quick. My current living situation was not an easy one.
Samantha's father and I had been divorced for five years. As I sat on the
subway looking around at the many faces of the day to day workers, the

ABC job was good for most people, but not me I was an entertainer. What else can I do with that in mind? I sat on the subway talking to myself. I had to pull something out of that magic hat I have used in my — magic! — Kid's! Kid's birthday parties! That's what I am good at! It didn't take me long. I kept visualizing birthday parties! Bam — *birthday parties!* Every year for Samantha's birthday I would always dress-up as a clown or some character and entertain her friends. I was funny and her friends loved it, especially when I was being silly. I truly love being silly. I can make believe better than anyone. Let's be honest if you really know me you know I never really grew up. Nor do I ever want to. I find children much more fun and interesting than adults. With my abilities I can give extraordinary birthday parties. I play piano and guitar. I can sing and play a mean kazoo! Zap! A new way to make a living!

I will someday emerge as one of the most well-known birthday party shows in town! I was going to give fabulous and expensive, no doubt, birthday parties to my fellow New Yorkers! Parents will love me!

That was the best subway ride I've ever had!

You need to know that I didn't give a $500 birthday party the following day. I had to find a venue for my super-duper birthday parties. I would find myself going to restaurants and apartments first. I remember my first character was Chuckles the Clown. I looked into what else clowns did at birthday parties. I found I had to get better face painting and magic. I bought a "how to" book for animal balloons. One bus ride home and I was a master. The people on the bus wished me luck as I exited! Waving their cats, dogs and giraffes!

Soon after I started giving parties I added a puppet show, including a collapsible stage. My friend Jo Ann from our 73st. day's asked her husband Mark to build my puppet stage. He was so good to me. I bought a keyboard to accompany my singing. At this point I have to give kudos to my mother for making me keep up with my piano lessons. Like every other kid, I wanted to be outside climbing trees with Kenny. So, thanks mom. You did prepare me for my next career.

The only place I could find to advertise was The New Yorker magazine. These ads cost a small fortune. But remember what Ted Turner always said, "Early to bed and early to rise and advertise!" Thank goodness for credit cards!

My daughter Samantha and I still laugh together remembering that first birthday party phone call. She listened carefully to my entire conversation. When I got off the phone, she gave me this astounding look.

"Mom let me get this straight. You told the lady you would charge $50 for the hour. You told her you were going to dress as a clown, bring the cake, party favors, and balloon animals. You continued with promising face painting, magic tricks, music and a puppet show. And did I hear, for 30 children?"

I stared back at my daughter — speechless!

"Not to mention you have to take a taxi to and from the party with all that stuff!"

"Did I say that? I remembered feeling so guilty asking for that amount, which really wasn't that much."

"Mom, you won't make any money — quick calculation — the lady will give you $50 and you will have spent $70 at least."

We both stood looking at each other — then rushed to each other for a big hug, laughing hysterically. How often do I have to say, thank heaven for children.

I did give that party. I did come and go in a taxi. I still have trouble understanding how I carried my puppets and puppet stage, a cake, (that could not be tipped over or squashed) party favors, keyboard, face painting and magic kit! Oh, yes, my clown outfit, I always dress and makeup my face up in front of the kids so they would not be frightened. Need I mention that was my first and only "$300 show" that I gave for $50! Remember I had to buy all the props for the show etc. Investment yes, but I didn't have the money. Once again, thank goodness for........!

Samantha and I went back to the drawing board and came up with a basic show (no cake, no party favors) and raised my party price. Thank you, Samantha, my lovely, fun loving, bright and beautiful daughter, (not too prejudice!) for your help and support at that time!

I was still Chuckles the Clown. I dress and makeup my face in front of the kids. I did a puppet show, sang with my keyboard, did some magic and face painting. Through 35 years I developed 7 different character shows, starting with Chuckles the clown. These were shows for children from 1 to 7 years old. I was then asked to make a show for kids 8 to 12. I still arrived as a clown but the birthday person got to throw a cream pie in my face at the end of the party. That was always a really big hit!

I managed to find a shopping cart with wheels that allowed me to trek up and down those specially sculptured subway steps and buses with all my props. (Once I imagined myself being *buried* with that cart!) When you reach your destination, you may be provided with a built-in workout as you pull your wheeled vehicle up and down tenement building stairs. (Yes there are five-story buildings with no elevators!) From one end of Manhattan Island to the other is about 13 miles. Do I have to point out that my parties were *not* usually around the corner? So my traveling time could run from 20 minutes to an hour. My show price eventually arrived at $180 for an hour party. The success of my clowning career was that I knew many children were afraid of clowns. And why wouldn't they? These strange colorful people looked bigger than life with their colorful costumes and colorful white painted faces. My solution! Arrive in my clown underwear!

I always dress and makeup my face in front of the kids. I was a mom like their moms, nothing to be afraid of. Engaging the children is imperative for success. I was not born with the gift of wanting to understand and love kids. I know that feeling of love grew out of me because I wasn't noticed or loved by my father. I really want to *see* the children and have them sense that. Being an actress makes it very easy because you have to be aware of what's going on around you all the time. It's a love trust combo. Many times a mother would come up to me and thank me for helping rid her child from the fear of clowns. I became known as the "underwear clown" for obvious reasons. The children giggled because I forget to dress. I discovered being silly worked for every single child's party. I have been clowning around for 36 some years. I am proudest of my ability to see and react with children of any ages.

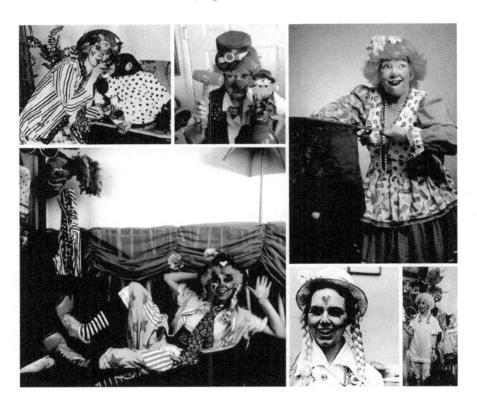

Doing a show for kids who were deaf, I hold as one of my best performances. I painted their faces, exaggerated my facial expressions, body movements did magic and stunts. It was like a silent movie — I got all smiles back! I also donated shows to various organizations that sponsored underprivileged children. Yes clowning was one of the highlights of my life. Laughing happy kids are one of the most beautiful things in life! With kids in your life there is always humor, lurking like a Jack-in-the-Box to give you an unexpected, wonderful laugh.

Remember my telling you about dragging my cart around subways and up and down tenement stairs? After a while I was able to take taxicabs became I became more successful. Remember I had developed 7 different shows. That being said, I would go to a party dressed as Matilda mouse, hail a taxi to get to the next party, then hop out looking like a Princess! As you can imagine changing in and out of costumes, bouncing around in the backseat and coming to instant stops in New York City traffic can be quite a trick. Preferably out of the cabdriver's view. The drivers were fascinated that I climbed in their taxi as one character, paid the fare as another! "Neat trick Lady!" And off they go!

One of my funniest (and expensive) moments with my mom's car occurred as I was racing to a party — perhaps not going the speed limit — and I went right through a red light. As I continued I kept looking for the big police man who had seen me run that light. But I didn't hear any sirens or see any flashing lights so — let's get to the party. Two weeks later I get a summons in the mail for going through a red light. Yes that red light! This is a mistake! No one pulled me over for running a light. I looked further into my summons, and there was a picture in black and white of a clown's face in the car looking rather guilty. (I believe I saw Jay Leno show it on his night time show! It was probably the only clown that ever ran a red light!) I had to admit that there were not a lot of Chuckles the Clowns driving around — I was on *Police Candid Camera.*! Humorous as it was, it did cost me.

If you're wondering why I would speed if I only had *one* show that day, I had a car now I could make three shows in a day. Timing became everything. And if you have ever driven in New York City traffic…need I say more?

I did have some more sobering situations being in costume when I was in my car. I arrived at my next party needing to change character. I parked a couple houses down from my party. Unknown to me there had been a series of robberies in that neighborhood. As I was changing, I noticed a woman pacing on her porch with her phone. She had an angry yet frightened look as she walked back and forth. Every now and then she would stop and look at me. I didn't really pay any attention I was too busy changing. I had just finished putting on the head piece of my Matilda mouse costume and there came a tap on my window — scared me half to death! I looked out as I put my window down and came face-to-face with a police officer! He was more frightened then I was. "Whoa! He jumped back. Keeping in character, I said in my best mouse voice, "Is there a problem officer?" (When you are in costume, you never break character.)

He literally took off his police officer hat and scratched his head. "Well, no I guess not now that I can see who it is. What are you doing, may I call you Miss Mouse?"

"Well, yes you may," — again in my mouse voice.

"Well, Miss Mouse," and he chuckled. "We've had some problems with break-ins in this neighborhood and you've seen enough movies to know that many times robbers will use facemasks to hide their identity. So what I'm asking is why are you disguised as —?"

I pointed out the window. "Over there at 4360 I am going to give a birthday party for their son and his friends."

The officer pointed to the woman who had stopped pacing on her porch. "That lady over there thought maybe you were casing the neighborhood." (Well, I was lookin' for some cheese!)

I laughed and yelled out the window to the lady saying, "I'm working a birthday party a couple houses away. Not to worry." I spoke to the officer one more time — in character — "you're not going to trap a lovely little mouse like me are you?"

His laugh was friendly as he walked away, "Not today, Miss M, not today."

So I didn't get picked up for casing the neighborhood. I got out of my car. I reached the front door of my party. Before I could ring the bell or knock, a tall, skinny teenager wearing an attempt at growing facial hair flings open the door. He looks me up and down and in a nasty tone asked, "So, are you the rat?"

I moved my head forward almost mouse nose to teenage nose, "No I am not the rat! I am the mouse. And you can cut me some cheese and show me to the party!" He just stared wide-eyed.

One scary time, I was stranded on the side of the highway standing by my car smoking like a campfire. I notice a truck pulling off the highway just in front of me coming to a stop. Here I was, dressed like a princess, wearing lovely satin heels, a peroxide wig and a gorgeous cream-colored lace dress. Two young good looking men leave the truck cab and start walking toward me. My first reaction was fear. I felt my stomach start to knot up. I relaxed a little when I saw them smiling broadly. When they stopped in front of me, I fumbled for some opening words and came out with —"Uh, hi, I'm a princess!"

Not missing a beat, and laughing heartily one of them answered, "Yeah and I'm a prince!"

We all had a laugh. I told them why I was dressed like that.

"Okay, Cindy, whatever you say"! These two were the good guys. One of them said something like if my mother or sister was stranded on the side of the road he would hope someone would stop and help. There were no cell phones during this time so they kindly drove me to a car repair garage. "Next time Cindy, you better pick a better pumpkin!" and off they drove.

If I knew where these two guys were now, I would bake them some brownies with walnuts and chocolate chips and send them a large batch. Better yet a pumpkin pie!

I finally discovered the perfect venue for my birthday parties. It was a brownstone building on the upper west side of Manhattan. It was nice to have the parties come to me. I was getting tired of driving and lugging my show around, not to mention the packing and unpacking. The hour and a half party cost $500 and it included everything, even a video of the show. I called my place of business, The Chuckles Fun House.

One morning, at the fun house, I was just preparing a party for 35 kids, when my stepfather George called. My mother had just died. Shocked and with great pain in my heart, I realized I still had to go on with the party,

35 children were enter the room. I simply had to push my emotions aside. I remembered that was the hardest thing I ever had to do. I almost lost it a couple of times during the party. I then had to travel to New Jersey for a house party. Samantha had arrived at the fun house to help me. I told her she couldn't let her feelings out until the next party was over. Once we exited the party, we both broke down in tears. My mother's death was extremely difficult for me. It took me over 3 years to come to terms with it and accept her death. One can accept but it never really goes away.

Even in heaven, my mom was thinking of me. My step father, George, gave me my mom's car. She wanted to make sure I didn't have to schlep up and down the steps of building, buses, and subways anymore. Thanks, mom, I sure do miss you. The Christmas clown below is Donna, my friend.

CHAPTER 15
My Singing Telegrams

As a single mom my birthday party business was keeping food on the table and a roof over our heads. Even so, I could not stop thinking about new ways to perform. I missed my adult audience. I wanted that audience back. And I wouldn't mind making a little more money.

As you know since I was very young, I loved being in character and performing. I loved to entertain and hear applause and laughter, and if appropriate, sometimes the hope of seeing tears of laughter. I had tapped my creative mind with Chuckles the Clown birthday parties. How could I become an entertainer for adults?

Something started to take root — Chuckles the Clown and adults. I was always asked to do adult birthday parties. Could I put these two things together into a performance, like a singing telegram perhaps? Back then singing telegrams were a big thing. Many of them focused on man and female strippers. Could Chuckles strip for adults? Chuckles, was silly and humorous for kids. What brand of silliness could I perform for adults as Chuckles in a singing telegram?

I let this question heat up on the front burner for a few days. And then — idea — what did I do with my kids? I arrived in my underwear. Clown, — underwear, — stripper? Keeping with the times the whole idea came together. I was going to be a clown stripper! My new business name became, "The Clown Around Stripagram" for special events in adult lives, birthdays, anniversaries, retirement, the list was endless!

Great idea but, how was I going to be a clown stripper? I was not about to really strip but how could I strip as a clown and still make it funny? Okay, why not start as a clown and strip down to my clown underwear — the reverse I had done for kids' parties. My excitement grew. I knew I had something. But was it funny enough for adults? The old learning curve returns. I knew that stripping to my clown underwear was humorous, but would it be funny enough to replace a voluptuous stripper? No, it was not enough to only do a clown strip down to my clown underwear. There was nothing really sexy involved.

Nevertheless, I had developed the confidence in my ability to create a new angle or perspective about what I was trying to do. I knew that while I was in performance, my mind would reveal something new in the stripagram world that would resemble a strip, but also be humorous.

I remembered that at the 7-12 year old parties I always ended my show by getting a cream pie thrown in my face. That was always a big hit with the older kids. Why couldn't I add the pie to my stripagram performances somehow? I went to work creating my costume and props for my new business, knowing full well I would be able to, throw in a "pie" somewhere!"

I needed a basic piece of underwear that would be humorous and cover my body. I bought a red and white striped leotard. I sewed bright red tassels on the breast area. I stuffed enormous falsies in my bra. Finally, displaying my total absence of taste, I cut a bright frosted brown wig to resemble a gross patch of pubic hair that I attached to the crotch of my leotard.

(Oh my, am I really going to do this?) I covered the entire outfit with a man's jacket and trousers. Now we needed some music. You know my love for music. I complemented my strip costume with a very unusual and silly musical instrument called a boomba. I had one made for me when I observed a boomba group performing in Pennsylvania. The boomba was designed to hold several instruments attached to a pogo stick. Starting with a cymbal at the top, followed by a cow bell, wood block, bicycle bell, large orchestra horn, wash board and tambourine attached to it. I am a one woman band, as I pump the pogo stick up and down with one hand — play the instruments with the other hand, then use a drumstick to hit the cymbals, the cow bell, then going up and down the wash board, ending with the bicycle bell and horn. Wow! Who's not going to love that?"

The choreography was next. I decided to play the boom-baa, while singing happy birthday (many times I wrote original songs but that's another story) to the client. Putting the boomba aside, I put the kazoo in my mouth and hum the typical sexy strip song.

A kazoo is a musical instrument about the size of a harmonica you put in your mouth. The person then hums as if to sing a song, humming.

While I am humming with the kazoo I perform the song, I dance suggestively around as I unbutton and remove my jacket to expose my leotard with two red tassels swaying as I move. I then start to unbutton my trousers while I focus on my client. With my trousers slipping down to my knees, (exposing the gross patch of frosted pubic hair) I would then take an empty pie tin and spray whip cream in it to make a birthday cream pie for my victim! As I dance closer and closer to them my trousers slip down even more, I pretend to trip, stumble, and my face would land right in the pie! I would certainly get into trouble if it landed in the clients face. Now all I need is a victim! Time to advertise!

The next picture shows me giving my brother, Jimmy, a pie in the face! I surprised him in Colorado one year for his birthday! Funny, he wasn't even sure it was me. (Sorry, I didn't include the strip.)

Booking my first stripagram was so exciting. But would I be able to pull it off? Apparently I did. Because the look on my first victim's face and everyone else's thinking he was really going to get a pie in the face and my getting the pie in the face was priceless! It brought down the house. When I tripped over my feet and my pants slid down to my knees exposing this gross frosted patch of pubic hair, I got a wild reaction — "Oh, gross!"

"What's that?" "Never in my life…." The people at the party would erupt with laughter. I was a success once again and I loved it.

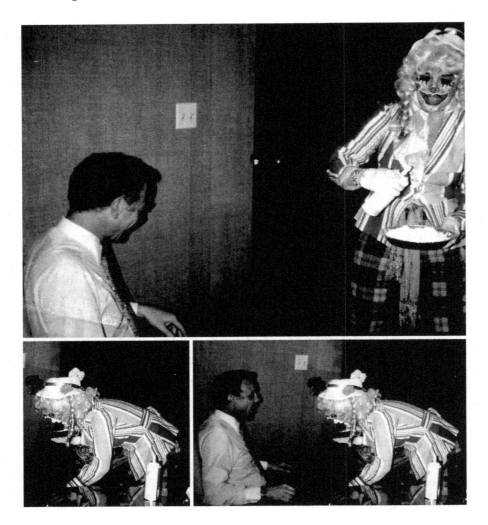

Once the laughter died down I gathered my props and got dressed. $75! for a 15 minute show, not bad. I stripped at restaurants, colleges, hotels and homes.

When the word stripper is floating out there, and I am a 45-year-old female, there is always a time for the unexpected, scary time. I was booked at a frat house in lower Manhattan. I could feel an air of disappointment that I wasn't a cleavage toting sex object. I heard someone in the crowd yell, "I thought John told us we were getting a stripper and we get a clown!" Then a few boos. I knew I had better get control and fast.

I got their attention and said, "Your friend didn't pay enough for a real stripagram so I'm what you're going to get! Then a new kind of eruption came from the group. "Money? Well if that's all it takes, pass the hat guys! We'll get you money!"

This was not good! Think fast, Lanie. I tried to raise my voice above the din and said, "That's really not necessary, guys. Thank you but —" The hat was loading up with money. I felt I was in real trouble. This was a new experience that I had not expected nor ever received. I was at a total loss!

Thankfully, the person that hired me stepped in and said, "Come on now guys let the clown do her thing for Tommy. It's his birthday." As quickly as I could I began to sing happy birthday — I set a new record time for singing doing my dance playing my instruments and stripping. I was getting the whip cream pie ready when suddenly it occurred to me maybe Tommy should get the pie in the face? I did my bit, I walked forward and my pants fell to my knees. They saw my patch of pubic hair — many laughed and many groaned. I took another step, tripped and stumbled with my face falling into the pie. I then looked at Tommy's friends, gesturing with the pie.... should I give Tommy the pie in the face? A roar of, "Yes" rang out from the crowd! Tripping once again in his direction — Tommy got it right in the face! Success! Tommy getting the pie brought a huge applause. I could feel a new friendly atmosphere coming from my audience. A few came over and told me how funny it was. They gave me the entire hatful of money as a tip. As I left, one of them said, "Hey, "Clowney," come back again and we will pay you for a real strip! Okay?" I muttered something like thanks again, I'll think about it and out the door I went. I lucked out that time. I decided never to take another frat house. All frat houses are not the same.

A singing telegram company in the city had seen my ad in the New Yorker magazine and was looking for new performers for their singing telegram company. I had to write original songs about the person I was singing to. Of course I said, yes. You always take the job and figure out the specifics later. It turns out that writing original songs — lyrics and music — is challenging and fun. My daughter got a big kick out of all the different songs and all the different topics I had to write and sing about. She helped me as much as she could. She was quite good at writing lyrics.

My belief that activity breeds activity resulted from my Clown Around Stripagrams, and now I was working for a singing telegram company. Sometimes they supplied the costume I needed and other times they left it up to me. One time that is lodged in my memory was when I had to dress as a gorilla.

The bus driver surprisingly stopped for me and opened the bus door. In my, *everyone is an audience life*, I asked,

"Will you take a banana?"

A sigh of exasperation, "Funny, just put the token in the slot, please." I started down the aisle and heard the driver comment,

"And no swinging on the overhead handles!" People on the bus broke out into laughter.

There was a brief pause, and he capped his remarks with, "Everybody has to be a comedian."

The reaction of the people on the bus was classic. Generally, everyone was wary of me and vacated seats for me. Couple of younger guys laughed and said something they thought was funny.

My venue for this telegram was the hospital. I did take off my gorilla head as I entered the hospital. I didn't really think a gorilla costume was appropriate but that's what they wanted so here I was. By now I am feeling somewhat uncomfortable, as I passed patients in the hallways, but I needed the money. I secured the room number and went to that floor asking a nurse to help me find room #426. As we walked to room #426, I noticed the nurse had a very concerned look on her face. "You're sure it's room #426?"

"Yes I'm quite certain. I am supposed to present a get-well, singing telegram to the patient in room #426. Is there a problem?"

"That is Mr. Peterson's room and he is recovering from a major heart attack."

Now I was really worried. My client's friend was elderly and I was quite certain Mr. Peterson was also. His seeing a gorilla walking into his room might give him another heart attack. What was his friend thinking? I needed to figure this out — and quickly! I decided to keep my head under my arm, as I walked into the room singing my get-well-soon telegram. Mr. Peterson sat straight up kind of pale and definitely dazed. He had a look of what in the world is going on? I walked to the bed— not getting too close! As gently and friendly as I could, I said, "I hope I didn't scare you. Your friend, Jeff, thought you might need a little cheering up and asked me to dress as a gorilla. I thought it best if I removed my head." Thankfully, a smile formed on his face. He reached for my hairy paws, drew me closer, then put is two hands to his face in a praying position, and nodded.

"I did have a fright for a minute, dear. But your manner and singing were so charming, and your costume so silly, that I did totally enjoy it." He then leaned in and whispered, "Thank you for removing your head!" We smiled I laughed a little, as only a gorilla can and left the room.

As I left the hospital with my gorilla head under my arm, I felt happy that I was providing some unexpected enjoyment to someone who really needed it.

Have you ever been to the Plaza Hotel in New York City? Sounds and is a very *highfalutin'* hotel for a very wealthy clientele. This was another interesting singing telegram experience. I was to write a song about saying goodbye, we will miss you, come back soon. That was the gist of it. The one drawback was it had to be sent/sung at 7am. There aren't many people awake at that hour in a fancy hotel like The Plaza. Nonetheless, that's where I was to be and with my boomba no less. I was not looking forward to entering the Plaza at that hour of the morning. But money talks and I sing as I'm told.

As I entered the hotel, I was besieged by four security guards coming at me from all sides. Was I dressed for The Plaza? I certainly was — if I were going to a Halloween party! I stood there with clown face and costume. I was totally prepared to explain my mission — Room #343 Miss Johnson, for a singing telegram gentleman. One of the security people checked the name and room number then nodded his head.

"Yes, these people are leaving to catch a plane. Please be quiet as possible. Other guests are sleeping." I looked at my boom-baa — everybody looked at my boom-baa. Playing that strange instrument quietly was definitely going to be a challenge.

"Well that will be a bit of a problem gentleman. My boom-baa doesn't have a quiet mode. I will do the best I can." They proceeded to lead me to the room number that I had mentioned. I felt so safe with 4 security guards leading the way. They spread out around me as I knocked on room #343. Long pause. I knocked again.

Wait, waiting, more waiting — finally, the door opened a crack and a lady appeared in her nightgown — staring at the group of us. Which brings up the obvious question, how would you like to open the door at 7 am to find a clown and 4 security guards staring back at you?

"What's going on?"

"I have a singing telegram from Mrs. Johnson, your mother."

"Good heavens," she said, "at this time of the morning?"

"Mrs. Johnson said your plane left at10am and I should be here to catch you before you leave for the airport."

The daughter was struggling to be appreciative in her state of rude awakening. "What was your name again?"

"Chuckles the Clown."

"Well, Chuckles," she said. "Thank you very much. I think it best if I just tell my mom how nice it was for her to send you. I'm going to add that you did an outstanding job, and we loved it. You see our plane doesn't leave until 10 *pm* — not 10 *am*. Stay here a minute please...., Chuckles." She turned away briefly returning with a lovely tip. "Thank you again." She closed the door. The men and I just looked at each other. "Right this way, Miss Chuckles." They walked me to the exit.

"I was just thinking you guys have never heard a boom-ba. I could perform for you guys if you —" All four guards muffled a brief laugh. One held the door for me and out I went! That was my 7 am singing telegram at the Plaza Hotel in New York City. How fun is my life!

CHAPTER 16

Husbands One and Two

After the pre-Broadway tour concluded, I was unknowingly going to be introduced to my first husband. The company had returned home only to find out the show was *not* going to Broadway. One of the actors in the cast decided to have a farewell party. While at the cast party, Thomas, one of the actors introduced me to a friend of his. He was a tall, redheaded man with a deep mellifluous voice. We talked a bit and after the party he asked me for a date. At first I was reluctant to accept. I had just moved on from Dr. Ryan who wanted to date me in six months! Add to that the fiasco during the tour where the entire cast believed I was gay. On the plus side, however, he wasn't wearing a wedding ring. Still, was this really the right time for me to focus on a serious male-female relationship? I accepted the date.

He made a good first impression pulling my chair back for me at the restaurant. He was curious about what happened on the tour. Was it fun being an understudy? Was I disappointed the show would not be going to Broadway? Did I think in the future I would become a Broadway star? I was pleased to see he was interested in me. We talked for a while. During dessert he put his fork down, looked at me, and said, "Some of the cast members at the party told me that you were gay."

"Excuse me? What did you say?"

He looked embarrassed.

"What makes you ask me a question like that?"

"Thomas told me about you and —" Breaking in I said,

"So asking me out to dinner is your plan to teach me to go straight too?" I looked him straight in the eye, and with great emphasis I said, "I am straight and I am really getting tired of this!"

"I'm so sorry. I didn't mean to offend you. I wanted to be sure…."

"You wanted to be sure of what?" Poor guy, I smiled reassuringly. "Never mind, it's okay. I just hope this is the last time I have to tell someone I am straight! That being said, I could use a cup of tea with my desert please, thank you." I saw him give me a smile. I returned his smile with a nod. He then signaled for our server.

The evening ended with amiability on both sides. He said, "I would like to see you again.

We did see each other again many times, eventually leading to our marriage. Our daughter, Samantha, came along about a year later. Many of you know that marriage is the hardest job you will ever have not to mention raising children. Our marriage lasted 14 years. The divorce was difficult. I, as you know, was from a "broken home." I hated creating another broken home for my child. The divorce was one of the hardest decisions I ever had to make. I remember vividly what that was like for me and it was the last thing in the world I wanted for my daughter. It was even more important now to be there for her.

Samantha was a successful job recruiter and living in New York City when I met my second husband. He brought with him a son, Kyle. He was nine years old when we met. Kyle's mother had passed when he was four. Here was this beautiful golden-haired child, looking up at me wondering who I was. He and I were going to have our struggles but lots of love also, while I was with his father. I was in love with both of them. Kyle's father was such a fun-loving person. Father and son were both a breath of fresh air! Our years together were during my two businesses, the Clown Around

Stripagram, and the Chuckles Fun House. Our home was in New Jersey. I would travel to New York City three days during the weekend and work at the fun house, or do my stripagrams, rejoining my family the rest of the week. We had 10 good years together.

Leaving was more painful because I also had to leave Kyle. (Kyle is holding his dog shadow, in the above picture.) He was 20 at the time. We had a very loving mother/son relationship. I was so happy to be there for him during those early years. We still communicate. He surprised me one day, by mail, with a little story he wrote which included a picture of us on a hike. I have included it at the end of this chapter. I was truly moved by story and the love he was showing me years later.

I could not rid myself of the confusion of succeeding so well in my career, yet not being able to workout, a successful marriage. There was no role model to work from so I wasn't surprise. My mother was married 3 times, no help there. And my father, well we know about him, he was invisible, yet haunting.

When marital relationships reach the point of disillusion as it did in my first two marriages, I needed to believe in myself so as not to allow divorce to question reinventions of myself. Furthermore, I could not let the haunting of my father's non-relationship with me make me believe that I was the one not lovable in the failed relationships.

I had people asking for my autograph. I was making huge amounts of money as a female. Getting fan mail, hanging out with gorgeous men! Why did I continue to feel worthless? I was being *seen* by millions of people. But I was not being *seen, understood* or *loved* by that one person.

I was to remain single for 2 years, then….. Someone *saw* me.

I met Joe, my third husband.

Great Memories

By
Kyle Stocker for Lanie

Some things that were scary at the time,
leave great memories!
Kyle, looking at the hand thinking....
"Are you crazy, you could be swept away?"

Eric, looking at the hand and thinking....
"It is so freaking cold, that is mountain water!"

Billy, looked at the hand and thought....
"I am getting out of here!"

Leonie "Lanie" Norton
and Jim Norton

CHAPTER 17
The Last Time I Heard My Father's Voice

I was 18 years old. I was living in New Jersey with my mother and step-father. I hadn't planned this phone call. You can't plan something like this, the need just comes over you. I decided I needed to hear my father's voice. I hadn't heard his voice in eight years.

I went to a nearby phone booth. I opened the phone book. There were two Norton's listed. My parents had named my brother D-O-N-N. They added the last letter N to keep him from being a junior. Close by was Donald C. Norton, who is my father. I put in my coins and put my finger in the first hole to begin dialing. I let my hand fall to my side. I can't tell you what I expected if he answered or if someone got him on the line. After all it had been eight years never having heard from him. He had to remember me I was his only daughter but...

I lifted my hand again and dialed the number. Ring, ring....ring.

"Hello?" It was my father. I couldn't speak. I turned to stare through the phone booth window.

"Hello?"

It must've been 30 seconds.

"Hello?"

I hung up.

My father's leaving put my brother and me into a very difficult situation. He had remarried a flamboyant German woman, nothing at all like my mother. Soon after he married he called and wanted to see my brother and me. My mother was extremely hurt and angry at being left so abruptly, add this to the fact that he remarried rather quickly. My brother and I were put in a situation where we had to take sides and if we weren't on mom's side, put it this way — we lived with my mother! Any kind of communication with my father was a betrayal. So we never spoke to him again.

As the week after I made my first call was passing, I had thoughts about whether my father missed me or even ever thought about me. Of course, how could he miss me, if he didn't know me, or want to know me. I found myself back at the phone booth. I didn't dare call from home risking what my mother would think to be a betrayal.

This time when he answered, I said hello. He asked me if I had called last week and I said yes. He said I thought you had called. He told me he was waiting for me to call as he didn't want to pressure me. I was confused about that remark. Part of me wanted him to just resolve to see me because he missed me. The other part realized that maybe he was respecting my situation with my mother about seeing him. The upshot was we set a time to meet at his house.

A few days later I knocked on his door, he opened it, there he was a stranger. The ensuing silence between us was uncomfortable, there was nothing to say! He motioned with his arm so I would go into the living room and sit down. He sat down as far away from me as possible. He broke the silence by telling me he had a quart of gin every day because it gave him strong bones. A bottle of gin set on the end table along with his glass. He lifted his glass and said, "That's true, you know, that's true." (The last time I checked gin for improving the strength of my bones — never mind!).

I know I offered some kind of small talk. His wife, Urna, had prepared something for us to eat. She flitted around in a tightly fitted colorful dress, large dangling ear rings, very high heels, smiling and laughing nervously. She always called me, "Lanie Dahlink," in her German accent. Lanie darling, your father is this or your father is that. She was absolutely the most annoying person. I know that's not nice to say but she took my father away from me and made my mother cry.

All the while she was flitting around my father was looking at her with this sly grin on his face. Who was he? Who was this person sitting across the room? He sat there as if I had come to pay homage to him. Oh god, let's eat so I can go home. This was just so strange and they were so forced. And for the life of me why was she so in love with this man? I felt like a lifeless body sitting there. I'm sure I made up stuff to say because he wouldn't know the difference anyway.

We all sat at the dining room table to have the food Urna prepared. We all said things of no significance. The feeling around the table was very uncomfortable. I have to admit I wolfed my food and stood up to leave. I left not feeling very much of anything was accomplished between us. What did I think was going to happen? We just stood there at the door. I am sure I was hoping, he would say he missed me and that he loved me. (Dream on, Lanie.) I certainly did not hug him. He never leaned in to hug me either. My father had never hugged me when we were a family, why would he hug him now? We never hugged! I don't remember him ever kissing me good morning or good night either. All these thoughts crossed my mind. My feelings of anger and sadness are ignited as I am forced to remember my youth with him or not with him as was my reality. As I carried on with my life the days following, the entire visit faded into total non-remembrance. To say he remained a stranger to me is an understatement.

You might've guessed that I was not in a hurry to visit him again. He wrote me from time to time. There was nothing in the voice of his letters that had any feeling for me as his daughter. He started all his letters with "Lanie, dear" — is that what a father writes to his daughter? It just sounded creepy. When he spoke to me as a child, he would say, Lanie, dear. After eight years! I felt like I was reading some kind of canned letter from father to daughter that he had read somewhere or someone had told him about, like his secretary. His whole manner toward me came out with absolutely no sincerity, love or caring, that I thought a father would feel in a father-daughter relationship.

Nevertheless, I did feel obligated to invite him to my wedding with Samantha's father, several years later. But there was no way he was walking me down the aisle! My stepfather, George, guided me down the aisle.

A year after I was married, my father moved to Florida. I think we both understood there was no way I was going to visit. When Samantha was about 9 years old, I get a call from him telling me he wasn't well and could Samantha and I come down to Florida to visit him. By this time he was on his third wife, Judy. Erna had died of cancer. It only took him six months to find another woman to be his caregiver. In my few meetings with his wives, I was continually amazed to hear them tell me what a wonderful father I had and how much they loved him. Where do these selfless, care-giving women come from? I was always upset when he married time and again. Looking back I am sure the ladies were nice and happy to have a companion, as both their husbands had died. My favorite was Judy, his last wife.

Samantha and I did visit him for a short time. Judy was such a lovely person and seemed to enjoy our visit. I was glad I visited as we were to be close friends after my father died. My daughter and I would continue to visit her as time passed when she needed support in her later years. My father didn't deserve such a terrific lady.

My father's health, especially his liver, deteriorated to the point that Judy needed a break from the care-giving. She needed more than a break unfortunately she needed a quadruple bypass. My father was placed in assisted living which he despised, while Judy was in recovery.

A few months later I got a call from Judy whose son was having serious health problems. She needed to go to him. Could I come down to be with my father? I reluctantly said, yes because Judy was such a lovely person to me.

One night after I arrived, it was late and my father was in bed. I was saying goodnight, as I walked toward the door, when I heard my father say....

"Lanie, dear, why don't you come and lie down next to me on the bed?" The reaction, the shock, the weirdness invaded me immediately, taking me back to when I was 10 years old.

"Come on, you are my daughter for goodness sake! What can it hurt if you lie down next to me? I am dying."

In my late 40s, even though I was feeling the same old emotional reaction, the feeling was more of a discomfort than a fear. I was able to say, almost like a teacher disciplining a student,

"Dad, I am not comfortable lying down next to you. I'm going to stay right here. (I was standing somewhat close to his bed.) I'm not going anywhere."

His dying words for me were, "Lie down next to me!" That's it? I saw a father dying on TV last night and his last words were, "Sorry I wasn't there for you. You are a good son and I love you." Isn't that what most dying parents say to their children? I am not even going to go there. My stepfather said thank you to me when he knew he was dying. I have that memory and I know how much that meant to me. I will just hang on to that positive thought. That's what keeps us living and able to love.

My father became desperate, pleading he couldn't hang on much longer. I responded patiently and quietly telling him Judy will be back soon. If you cannot hang on, it's okay to let go. Everyone will be fine and Judy will be okay. I finally realized that all I was going to get from my father, was what *he* wanted. I admit I was angry inside doing my best to show patience and understanding outside. I continued telling him it was okay for him to let go if he needed to. I turned out the light and left. Judy returned the next day. As soon as I could I flew home. Not long after I arrived home, Judy called and told me that my father had died. The sad truth is after my father died, I felt nothing. Moreover, I had heard his voice for the last time.

So here I am flying back down to Florida for my father's funeral. The turnout for his funeral was far greater than my expectations. I also heard what a charming father I had, what a great sense of humor, how good he was to everyone. I stood there stunned — I couldn't believe who they were talking about! Were they really talking about my father? I discovered he had left me and my brother Donn $10,000 each. Confusing at first, but realizing, of course, if you cannot love, you can always make a show of it with money. I went away from the funeral understanding that he was a charmer. He didn't love me or any of these people he was just feeding his greedy ego. He certainly took a pass on loving my mother and his children.

I was 50 years old when he died. I had my last words with him, but was he still going to prey on my mind for the rest of my life. Would I ever be able to see his face sitting on his lap at five years old?

CHAPTER 18

Goodbye New York City

I was 60 years old. I was clowned-and-birthday-partied-out! I had left my second husband. My daughter Samantha had married. She and her husband had excellent jobs in New York City as personnel recruiters. They were building a lovely life for themselves as a married couple and started to form their own recruiting business, The Talent Magnet.

As I thought about leaving New York, I began telling people my plan to relocate to Los Angeles. I didn't really feel especially needed by anyone. As I just mentioned, my daughter was fine with her new husband, and she was all I really cared about except Kyle my stepson. She said she would miss me, of course, but I should go and find that new life waiting for me out there. My stepfather, George, who I was living with after I left my second husband, told me I had a life to live so, go for it! He lived with a lovely woman named Katrina, who was assisting him with some life-needs because of his age, and they were doing well together. She became part of the family and we became good friends. Katrina really cared for my father. My whole family was grateful for the loving ways she responded to him. I would miss her but I needed to move on. Many of my friends were envious and admired my courage at the age of 60, to start a brand-new life. Not to mention driving all alone to the other side of the country.

Decision made! I was leaving for LA as soon I had everything set up for my arrival. A friend of mine was arranging an apartment for me on the beach. My furniture, limited as it was, would be sent ahead. I was so busy and excited. I didn't have time to be frightened of completely relocating — with nobody I knew out there and no real prospects of a job in the entertainment industry or anywhere else!

The day came for my departure. My travel-time estimation was three days to LA, stopping at motels on the way. My lovely brother, Donn, had bought me a new Honda for my trip. He also negotiated a way out of my lease at the brownstone, in NYC where I did the birthday parties. My landlord ended up paying me to leave the apartment so he could start renovating and raise the rent, resulting with me on my way to LA with about $20,000 in my pocket and a brand new car. My brother Donn worked his magic. I was truly blessed with two wonderful and loving brothers.

My brother Donn, guess who?, and his wife Paula, on our way to lunch in, Hoboken, NJ.

My suitcase in my car, two large stuffed animals, two large cut plants in a bucket of water and a very large stump of a tree (don't ask) finally, I am in my car with clean panties and toothbrush in top shirt pocket. I didn't want to have to take my suitcase into every place I stopped for the night. I started my car. I had a day's ride in front of me. I pulled onto the highway and pressed on!

That first day of travel gave me such a feeling of rebirth and freedom. I really wanted to just think of myself. I had given back so much in my life to others, I needed to give back to me.

I woke up in my cozy hotel room the next morning. One day down. The second day toward my new life took my hand. My new little Honda and I were....

As Willie Nelson would say, "On the road again"

I focused on being as excited as I had been yesterday, keeping my eyes and my thoughts forward.

As my car turned onto the entranceway of, route 80 West, the universe must have been in touch with my excitement and anxiety leaving NYC, a billboard appeared with huge letters shouting, "*Vote for Norton*!" The hair stood up on the back of my neck. I felt goose bumps all over! "*Vote for Norton*" blazed joyfully across my heart! My first spiritual experience, wait a minute! Was I kidding myself? Crazy coincidence or...? As my little Honda crested the hill in front of me, an especially glorious rainbow blanketed the sky! I was confused. Wasn't a rainbow prompted by rain? Where was the rain to cause the rainbow? I pulled off the first safe place I could leave the highway. I got out of my car and looked behind me, not a cloud in the sky! I looked as far as I could see in front of me beyond the rainbow — totally free of clouds! How in the world could there be a rainbow with no rain anywhere? I had just seen the billboard "*Vote for Norton.*" Now I am seeing an amazingly perfect rainbow with no rain. A unique feeling of giddiness enveloped me as I settled back behind the wheel. The rainbow had now curved perfectly so that my highway and my little Honda went through and under it! My rainbow tunnel — I obviously had a pot of gold coming to me in my LA future!

Coincidence? No! Not on your life! These extraordinary phenomena were *no* coincidences! Whatever is *out there* or *up there* was comforting me, signaling me that I was on the right road to a new home. I yelled out, "OK, mom. I got it. I got it!" Laughing, I said, "Over and out!"

At that point my life changed to understand that perhaps in the past I had been missing signs like these. As my life continued, I learned to see many signs that told me about my reality. Ever since my mother passed, I would find butterflies showing up in the oddest places, lightly and softly landing near me. The billboard and the rainbow made me realize that the butterfly was my mother telling me she was with me. I had missed that sign. I now vowed that I was never going to miss another. Los Angeles — here I come — be ready for me because I am going to *reinvent* myself in LA and collect my pot of gold! As I rode through my rainbow tunnel, I decided I was pretty happy with the woman that I had been over the last 40 years. I was so looking forward to what the next 30 years would bring me. Why did I let my father give me my worth? I remain undaunted.

CHAPTER 19
Hello LA

I pulled into the parking lot of my new apartment my friend had arranged for me. The place was in Marina del Rey, California. Not a large place, two-rooms, balcony view of the bay and a path to the beach out my front door. My apartment was on the bay which afforded me a wonderful view of the sail boats going in and out of the ocean. I was right at the limit of what I could spend for an apartment and still eat and put gas in my car. At least I had a place to rest my weary head after a day's work. Our income plan was to make and sell our own soap. We were both kind of crafty like that.

I had a glorious time fixing up my little home with earthy things I would find on the ground. Large fallen palm branches stretched across my balcony. Sea shells and rocks were spread on top of any service I could find. The glow of candles, were seen every night from my new home. I was just a hop, skip and a jump from the ocean. I had always wanted to live, "By the sea, by the sea, by the glorious sea!" A fun song to make me smile and feel at home!

I decided I would find a job while waiting for my friend to start the soap business. After discussing the way we would make the soap and other issues concerning the sales, it never materialized. I was on my own. I was better reinventing myself alone anyway, so no problem.

My first job was with an entertainment company. Apparently, I was getting to much business for the owner and he didn't want to work that hard. He fired me and hired young girls. That lasted a month or so. Next I took a job in a retirement home. I didn't realize how physical taking care of the elderly is — helping people get in and out wheelchairs, moving them to the other side of the bed, changing diapers for adults. I was pretty much on my feet for my entire shift. I quickly understood this was not going to work and gave my two week's notice. I saw many previously famous people, while working there, who had no idea who they had been and no idea who they were now. I would approach them mentioning how I always enjoyed their performance, no response was given. My heart would sadden for them.

I thought maybe I should have some male company and started dating a friend of a friend. He was another man who wanted my role in his life to be making him feel good about himself. Older men are just as much ego-oriented as any other age male. He had his own set of problems and I didn't want to go there.

Christmas time was rolling around. Six months had passed and I realized I didn't like living alone, and my money was quickly running out. It had been a year after leaving my second husband. One thing I knew I didn't have to worry about was a white Christmas in California. I was on my balcony looking out at the bay. The evening was quiet and beautiful — lights were sparkling all over my neighborhood — in front of me stood a giant Southern California Christmas tree.

There was a lovely breeze off the bay cooling me down from the day's previous heat. I turned my gaze to the stars feeling lonelier than I had ever felt. I stood up and into the vastness of the nighttime sky. "Hey, out there I know I have had two husbands already and you might think I am a bit greedy, 60 is not dead, it has been a year and I am really lonely, can you come up with one more?"

I heard myself loud and clear. I started to laugh. That's not exactly how you are supposed to pray! I realized that I had to make a dedicated attempt to find real love in my life. I continued my monologue to the universe, "I want to love a man who wants to love me. I don't care what he looks like, I know looks don't matter. I want a man of character and integrity. I want a man to be partners with. We both have to be able to *see* each other. No man has ever seen me." I closed my eyes, stood very still, hoping for some sign. I hadn't experienced any more "signs" since I arrived in California.

Longing for some snow and my daughter, I flew back for Christmas. While I was in New York City visiting my daughter, I thought about one of my favorite psychics who once had read for me. What have I got to lose! I called that psychic. What would she see in my future this time? While drawing big circles over and over on paper with her sharpened pencil, she spoke! There is a man in your future. This person you are seeking will have five things about him you must discover — he is Republican, his family will love, he will have a scar on his chest, experience with boats and the ocean, and the two of you will have great sex! She then revealed the date I would meet him, March 17, 2004. At the time of the reading it was December, 2003 so my search began.

Maybe my friend and I couldn't make soap together but we could search for men. We joined the Volunteer Coast Guard for the sole purpose of meeting men! Good place to start. When you reach 60 years old, there is no time for games! I had one purpose at the Volunteer Coast Guard. I had only two "ask-able" questions since their connection with boats and the sea was obvious. Are you a Republican? Do you have a scar on your chest? Do you have children? Beating around the bush was not an option! I was totally brazen with every man I met at all the Volunteer Coast Guard activities.

Just before New Year's, we went to a Volunteer Coast Guard Ball. I was task oriented, I must've danced with at least 10 men asking them the three questions that were "ask-able." Are you Republican? Do you have a scar on your chest? Once again as my mother would always say… "It's never easy!" If I got a Democrat, he would have a scar on his chest. If I got a Republican, he would not have a scar on his chest. I don't know if it was my last attempt or not, but one guy, who unfortunately looked really good to me, said the following, "I'm not a Republican. And I don't have a scar on my chest. But for you, right now, I will cut my chest to create a scar and register as a Republican as quickly as I can!" He had a big smile on his face. I know I had a big smile on my face. We broke into laughter, gave each other a hug and went our separate ways. The closest I ever came was 4 out of 5. Wondering what happened? He was gay. At least at this age I knew what that meant, and we both laughed! We became fast friends after that. He even volunteered to help with the search.

Hit or miss was not working. I realized I had to try a different avenue. The on line dating service was just starting in those days. I thought, why not? I choose eHarmony; it was suppose to be the best. Of course I had more than one picture of myself. So I put up a picture and a profile and waited. The first response I get was a guy who didn't look anything like his picture. Go figure! The next man who answered was 85! I liked his profile, but he said long walks on the beach were out. Oh well, moving on.

Frustration! But — too soon to give up! Earlier I had received a profile that I liked but there was no picture. After all I did say looks don't matter. No further responses had stimulated me so I retraced my steps to my no picture guy. Take a chance, I said to myself. I needed some kind of activity in my search. I sent a text to him on a Friday. More frustration, I waited three days for a response. Finally, he answered me by phone on Monday. I immediately loved the sound of his voice. I told him I wanted to drive up and see him. I could be there in about an hour. He spoke again.

"It's more like an hour and a half to Temecula. My, you are certainly impulsive!" He spoke with a very calm and soothing tone, very manly. I loved the feeling that came over me when I heard his voice.

"If it's okay, I have the time. I would really like to drive to Temecula and meet you right now."

"Okay. Fine with me but by the time you get here there won't be anything open really."

"Well if you don't mind booking me in a hotel. I could stay the night."

"No, I don't mind. Okay, whatever you want." I didn't know then, but, "whatever you want" was going to be a phrase he would say often.

I can still feel the excitement run through my body. How much fun is this? I'm 21 again, and I can do anything I want!

Temecula, California was incorporated in 1989. The city lies about an hour and half east of Los Angeles in the inland valley. The interstate available to Temecula was straight through dark mountains the whole way, no highway lighting. I left the bay area that night. Fortunately the moon was out a bit, helping me see both sides of the highway, as I had many curves and turns through the dark mountain roads.

Every 15 minutes I would stop and call Joe, his name was Joseph Pytlak. He would answer, and I would try to tell him where I was according to his directions. Apparently I was going in the right direction because he said just a little while longer every time I called.

I came out of the mountains and civilization reappeared. The turnoff for Temecula came into view, and I pulled off to call Joe. He told me to call him again when I was in that city itself, and he would direct me to the hotel. He would meet me there.

Remember I'm a city girl. We don't have any mountains in New York City. I don't know where West is — or any direction for that matter. I learned from my mother to say next door, up the highway, down the highway, across the state. Joe kept telling me about East and West and North and South with a lot of left and rights in between. Of course, he was a sailor! I was very worried that I would look like an idiot and lose my way.

I tried to follow Joe's directions when I reached Temecula, unfortunately I found myself lost, frustrated, and embarrassed next to a very dark, no-longer-in-business restaurant. I called Joe and he said turn around and there will be your hotel. I turned around and Joe was right. I checked in, went to my room, and began fixing myself up for my first impression. I put my favorite pirate puffy-sleeved blouse that I thought was rather sexy. Now my skirt, I slid into my cute short, maybe slightly too short for a 60-year-old, skirt with brightly colored flowers, I still wore stockings. I shuffled on sandals in case he lied about his height. Oh dear, what was I to do with my face? I stared into the mirror trying to find out what Joe would see. If he wasn't lying, he was five years younger than me. Was I too old to pull off a sensational impression with a younger man? Women have so many things to worry about! As I was staring into the mirror, the hotel phone rang. Joe was waiting for me downstairs in the lobby. The camera had been good to me in my youth. How was my *real* face in my old age? I decided to stop making so much fuss about everything being so perfect. I went for my powder and lipstick. Done! I did the best I could with my hair. This is me, and if Joe doesn't like me, that's his problem. Liar, liar, pants are on fire! Anyway, who knows, I may not like him either. I started to realize he was also making a first impression.

I stood in the elevator ready to face the man I had just driven an hour and half to see. The elevator doors parted, and I walked out with my perhaps too short skirt into the lobby. We both spotted each other simultaneously. We knew immediately who each other was. Was I wrong, or did his face reveal he liked what he saw? He stood 6 feet tall in his blue jeans. He hadn't lied about his height. He held his baseball cap with the name of a US Navy ship across the front of him. His gray hair cropped closely around his face. He was wearing a light blue windbreaker over a soft brown shirt. He wasted no time advancing toward me. When he reached me, he stopped and exclaimed, his face glowing with a smile, "You are so beautiful!" I know that I was beaming at him. I reached down and took his hand. I looked down to see our hands clasping — what an exquisite tingling all up and down my arm! I can still feel it running through my being like it was yesterday!

His gentle hazel eyes knocked me out! I had heard those words before, but never so sincerely and gently. We were like all those nervous couples just meeting each other in the movies, the entire audience can feel the romantic attraction and connection. This time I was experiencing the connection myself — and I was not in a movie!

Joe immediately took over the conversation. "I wanted to get you something, but I didn't know what you might like. A lady at work suggested what she would like if she were you." He laughed slightly. He was so emotional he ran out of breath. He inhaled noticeably. He continued, "I'd like you to have this. I hope you like it." He handed me a little white box with the red ribbon tied around it.

I was so touched I could hardly speak. Here's a younger guy wanting to buy a present for a 60-year-old woman he doesn't even know! And on a first blind date! Is all this happening? This guy is so different — in such a beautiful way! I fumbled as I untied the ribbon, almost dropping the box. I took off the lid to discover an adorable little stuffed bear with a pink bow blossoming from his neck. I finally spoke, "Oh, Joe, how sweet of you!" There was also a card. It read, "Thank you for sharing a moment in time with me." I held it the bear and card close to me, smiled and said thank you. He seemed so pleased.

We got in his truck to go to the casino in town as that was the only place open this time of night available for any kind of food. He opened the car door for me every time we had to get into or get out of the car. I was so impressed — an old-fashioned gentleman. (And after 16 years of marriage, he is still a gentleman and still opens the door for me everywhere.) What a lucky 60-year-old woman. After two attempts at marriage that didn't work, could I be approaching a relationship where love flowed from both sides?

We had to walk a little way to the casino after parking the truck. We kept bumping into each other walking through the parking lot. We couldn't seem to keep away from each other. We walked with his right hip and leg seemingly attached to my left hip and leg. It appeared as if we were kind of glued together step after step after step. Kind of corny, but felt so good and wonderful! We went into the bar and ordered cranberry juice. We sat and talked and talked and talked and forgot to drink our juice. I think it was about one in the morning when the bartender hinted around that he would like to close up and go home. We looked around the place and sure enough we were the only ones still there at the bar area in the casino. The bartender finally said, "You two can sit there as long as you want, but I'm closing up, and, oh yeah, all those juices you had," we only ordered one apiece we got so busy talking, "They're on the house!" We just laughed! I had a feeling the bartender knew that we were just meeting and were doing very well. We started to leave. Joe left a nice tip on the table. We went out the door.

Joe had a blue pickup truck. He drove us to my hotel. The minute he started driving I pushed myself as close to him as I could. I happen to love kissing and I was wondering how it would feel kissing each other. Is that same electricity between us going to continue? I threw a leg over him and faced him on his lap. He was startled, but he didn't stop me. Kissing! That's what I always did best.

We both started feeling the late hour, especially me after my long drive. He walked me to my hotel room, perhaps expecting to be invited in after our kissing session. I made the decision that was as far as we were going to go. I thanked him for a lovely time and asked him about tomorrow. As it would be Sunday, he told me he would take me out for breakfast. We would then spend the day together.

I was wondering if last night had been a dream or was there still going to be something between us in the morning. Wondering over, we had a lovely kiss hello and a reassuring hug. The chemistry was still there. We had a nice breakfast. Afterwards, I followed him in my little green Honda as we made our way to his home nearby. We pulled into the driveway of a beautiful two-story home, three bedrooms, family room, screened in porch and a little add-on barroom with colored lights, wine rack and barstools. We went outside to view a pool and a spa. We have electricity between us and now, we have a pool and a spa and a really beautiful home! Is this too good to be true?

We went back in the house for a bite. He got some sandwich makings out of the refrigerator sat down next to me on a barstool. He took my hand, looked me straight in the eye and said, "I don't know about you, but I'm not going to be looking for anyone else."

I was not prepared for him to make such a quick decision. I know he wanted an answer, but I had failed twice badly in former marriages and dodged an answer. I squeezed his hand lovingly and said, "I would love to jump in the pool with you, and then maybe we could make the sandwiches later." He took the hint and changed subject. He said I could do whatever I wanted to do but he wasn't going to look for anyone else.

We had fun in the pool and the spa. Forget the sandwiches, Joe cooked some steaks on the grill outside and I cooked asparagus inside. Dusk was falling and the question of my staying overnight came up. He offered me a bedroom upstairs if that would be my choosing. Things were feeling so good yet so different at this point. I told him I liked to dance. Joe put on some music from one of his cd's. Love was in the air. There was something between us I had never felt before and not easy to describe. I am now going to admit with no apologies to throwing the make-him-wait, good girl to the winds — we made love.

Just for fun let's see how well I have done with my five questions. He already stated he was a Republican in his profile on eHarmony. He had been in the Navy 28 years. That probably has something to do with ships and the sea! He had a daughter and a granddaughter he told me would love me. And making love with Joe was wonderful. So where was the scar on the chest? 4 out of 5 and not gay, that's great!

When I awoke the next morning, I felt like a princess in a beautiful castle. I decided to share my psychic's premonitions with Joe. When I divulged the 5 requirements for my one and only true love, a strange look appeared on Joe's face. (Not a big believer I guess.) During our time in his pool we would search for the scare. After a while he remembered a small scar on his chest that he got while training to go into the Navy. Bingo! It's him! I continued to live at Marina del Rey, but began to spend more and more time with Joe at his home.

Here is a fun story about the spirit world that goes with our romance and marriage. Joe knew I was an actress in my past. Many years before, I was 27 at the time he saw my "ring around the collar commercial." In that commercial there was a moment I looked up at my husband with loving eyes and say, "You will beat him this time dear, because you don't have ring around the collar!" He told me when he saw the commercial, he said to himself, how wonderful it would be to have a woman look up at me, lovingly like that. He took both my hands, and again looking at me lovingly said, "And here you are a beautiful woman and looking at me with loving eyes — amazing!" He had me on that one! That day we started making plans for my moving in with him.

So my thoughts to you are, it's never too late to find love. I did luck out, but maybe I didn't. Maybe you can have a different way of doing it. Maybe you will find the love that you are looking for. Good luck, if you are in that neighborhood of your life. Our next anniversary is July 2, 2021, 16 unbelievably amazing, fun loving years as husband and wife!

CHAPTER 20
My Life with Joe

I had just run out of money living in California. Both jobs had fallen apart. I could no longer afford my apartment. What's my next move? Obviously move to a cheaper place. Wait a minute — my brother Donn, just bought a condo in La Quinta, the Palm Springs California area. Maybe I could live there, be the overseer to ensure its safety. After all he and his wife, Paula, wouldn't be staying there very often as they lived out of state. I knew he had bought it as an investment and probably would be selling it soon as the market was good. He told me he thought that my being the overseer was a great idea. It was a win-win — I would have a place to live — he would have free security. Donn is always there for me whether it's advice, money, or brotherly love.

It had been four months since Joe and I had met and things were going very well. Now we spent our time between La Quinta and Joe's home in Temecula. Playing house at two fabulous places was certainly enjoyable. For the first time I had a man who I felt saw me as a partner rather than someone to feed his ego. On July 2, 2005 we got married.

Joe had a comfortable pension after 28 years in the Navy. I had money coming in every month from SAG and AFTRA, from my acting pensions.

Joe didn't want me to work. He was happy to pay all our bills. Wow, that was a first.

As time went by and our relationship strengthened, I began to miss performing. Chuckles the Clown was always in my repertoire. I did some research and found an agency that would get jobs for me. Donna, the owner of All Ways Entertainment, put me to work and also taught me how to improve my face painting for the children's parties. She is an amazing artist. My new clown name was Giddy Gertie! Then I became Zanie Lanie! Donna took me to clown conventions where I took courses in balloon sculpture and instructions in performing clown skits. At the 2017 West Coast National Clown Convention in LA, I won first place for face painting and my original clown skit also won first place. It was a great day. You can see the skit on: (youtu.be/ifXop1d7ntU) I pretend to be a French waitress, in clown attire.

I still had time and energy for more activities. My love for children sent me searching for a teaching job. In California I had enough credits to qualify as a substitute aide for special education teachers. Birthday parties on the weekends and teaching during the week, kept me busy and happy for 3 years. Then something drew me to my neighbor, Wendy. She was making fancy water and wine bottle covers with fabric and feathery colorful boas. She was doing very well but wanted to expand. That's right! I joined her. I may be in my 70's but I act like the energizer bunny! We met a wedding planner who wanted us to use the same kind of stretchy and fun material with boas for fascinator hats and wedding hats. Wendy decided she had enough work with her wine covers, so I took over the hat business.

I have included a selection of hats from Babe Hayes Originals, which I designed and created. I named the company after my mother. She was a model and everyone called her "Babe."

Joe helped me find some material samples online that would be appropriate for wedding hats. The material arrived. I got out my glue gun and sewing machine and, voila! — A wedding hat! The first one I designed sold for $ 145.00. Joe couldn't believe it! Other wedding planners and women's clubs heard about my hats, and Wendy's wine covers. For five years we had a good creative business. We were very popular at all the summer and winter events.

I was really happy substitute teaching, clowning and making fascinator hats. Life with Joe, my work and businesses were something I never expected but certainly welcomed.

Eventually we decided we didn't need the large two-story house in Temecula. Too much to clean, we weren't using the pool that much anymore, and the stairs became steeper as we got older. We moved to Hemet, California, buying a permanently anchored double-wide manufactured home on the highest point of the park. We now have an expansive view of the mountains off our front porch and spend many hours watching sunsets and weather moving in and out.

New place —new things to do! I was still clowning, and now selling my hats to a store adjacent to an art gallery in Hemet. As I passed the gallery one day, I noticed a sign mentioning art classes. I decided I wanted to learn to paint. I had painted children's faces for birthday parties, what else could I learn in terms of painting?

I joined the Hemet Art Association and started taking art classes. The added fun was that people who belonged to the Association could hang their work in the gallery. There was a judging once a month with ribbons and points given out. Betty, my water color instructor, is just marvelous and so talented. I discovered my love for watercolor while taking her class. I quickly assimilated techniques and applied them to the current project. I am also taking a water color collage class with Miyoko, a very talented Japanese artist. Both teachers have amazing teaching and artist credentials. I hung some pictures, won some prizes, and had a great time. I even became the Gallery Director for a year. The gallery became my second home and I loved working there with all the volunteers. We were like a little artist family.

These are my paintings, water color, acrylic and mixed media. Can you find Joe's rocks?

The Association also sponsored a Kids Art Jam class once a month. I looked into that activity and became the co-leader with Paula, another talented artist, for about three years. Our job was to set up an activity suitable for ages 6-12 at the gallery. The best part of this class was to watch these kids use their imaginations and take their projects to a totally different place, than I imagined. What a joy it was to bring art to these kids and get them to put down their computer games for at least an hour or two.

Enough about me, what about Joe?

Joe discovered rock tumbling from Wolf, the husband of a friend of mine. They live in Fly Creek, (You'll love *that* town!) New York. Joe and I were visiting my other friend, Gwen, who also lives in Fly Creek. We were all having dinner together. After dinner, Wolf took us down to his basement. He showed us his *one* rock tumbler. I emphasized one because, well....

Soon after we arrived at our new home in Hemet, Joe became an extensive lover of rocks. We now have *8 dual tumblers* running 24\7 in our dining room! Dual tumblers mean we have 16 tumblers in our dining room. There are no basements in a manufactured home. What? Oh no we're used to the noise. We really don't even hear the sound anymore. Besides, after two husbands.... Joe can do whatever he wants!

Joe had always supported me in everything I did, the rock tumbling became something that *we* did together. This hobby resulted in our fashioning key chains, refrigerator magnets and necklaces which we gave away freely wherever we went. We have thousands and thousands of beautiful shinny rocks, on every surface in our house. Kids in the neighborhood are constantly knocking on our door and asking to see Joe's rocks. We give out rocks on Halloween rather than candy! When Joe answers the phone he says, "Joe's rock shop! What's tumblin'?"

Life with Joe will always be fun and exciting because both of us are always ready to explore something new. Our love and understanding of each other always offers the opportunity for us to work together. Sharing your life with your partner is what brings meaning to your relationship. And now it appears we are working on my memoir together. It seems the joys of love are never ending. We are truly blessed.

CHAPTER 21

The Universe and Me

You may remember as I was leaving New York City to LA I saw some signs that something or someone was guiding me. I was comforted by a billboard — Vote for Norton — and a giant, arching rainbow facing LA. I believe these signs came from God, the Universe, or energy from passed family members. I can only bear witness to the loving energy and confidence it gave me as I recognized these signs. I wanted to read books about past life regression, after feeling someone was guiding me here. The idea of past lives greatly intrigued me and I decided to pursue it. I was very familiar with psychics and their world, but knew nothing about being hypnotized.

I discovered that certain professional hypnotists specialize in past life regression therapy. I did some research in my area and found a hypnotist that would work with you and your past lives. I made an appointment the next week. I was very excited and looked forward to being hypnotized, but could I be hypnotized was my question?

When I arrived at the practitioner's office, he had me lay down on a couch much like the psychiatrist office. He started to prepare me for hypnosis. I was told to close my eyes, relax and listen to his voice. He would tell me to take deep breaths, and go deeper and deeper into a peaceful place. When he felt I was sufficiently hypnotized he then asked me, "What do you see? Where do you think you are?"

Hypnotists can recover our past memories and past lives. All my experiences in past life regressions, ended with unpleasant deaths. I always died so young.

In one of my past lives I was 16 years old riding in a horse show. My horse missed the hurdle, stumbled and through me off! I broke my neck. I found myself floating above my dead body watching my family and friends below in tears clutching my body. They looked sad but I didn't feel any emotion. I was amazed at what I saw and how I felt.

The next session I found myself at a very significant place. I was in a very dark small wooden cabin, where I was dressed totally in black sitting looking out a window at mountains covered in snow. I was a child of seven. I was completely covered in a long black dress and a thin black cape. I couldn't stop shivering. I got up to perhaps find a warmer place to shelter myself and found the door locked! I grew colder and colder until a strange woman, also dressed totally in black, opened the locked door. Her hooded cape covered her face. She walked toward me pointing her finger accusingly, screaming, "You are a sinner a sinner a sinner! And you know how you sinned, you horrible child! You can't fool me! You're going to stay in this room alone until you die!" She turned away, walking out the door, and locking me in. How had I sinned? How? Am I really going to die in this room alone? Then I heard myself gasp and cry out still under hypnosis "I slept with my father! I slept with my father! Oh, my god, I slept with my father!" I am crying — time passed. No food no water for days. I am very weak. I watch myself crawl hopelessly toward the door. I have no strength. Complete silence, cold dark silence — I die.

Thank goodness the hypnotist spoke to me in my hypnotic state, opened that locked door and took me outside. He then led me to a beautiful place where I sat on rocks with multiple rainbows, warm sunlight, and waterfalls surrounding me. You are warm! You can stay there and rest and heal. You are at peace.

A spooky aftermath of my past death, in the cabin where I died, was a road trip my husband and I took soon after that session. We came across a sign pointing "WATERFALL." Like most people we both love waterfalls. We got out of the car to find the waterfall. There seemed no obvious path to this promised waterfall. We were just about to give up when several young people bent their way out through bushes ahead of us. We asked them if they had seen the waterfall. They said yes and pointed through the bushes where they had just come from. They offered to take us to the waterfall, but we told them thank you anyway and parted our way through the bushes. Immediately, I heard the rush of water. I was a little ahead of Joe. I could see a series of rocks worn like steps going up the side of a wide hill allowing water to cascade down the rocks. I looked down to see where the water fell into the stream. The sun was shimmering through the trees around us. I began to cry softly. I felt a familiar warm feeling come over me. I can still see that place and experience the familiar feeling that it brought out of me. Joe came up beside me asking me if I was okay. I turned to him, hugging him deeply. I told him I know this place — I have been to this place before. Joe looked confused. I reminded him about my experience dying in the cabin and then taken to a waterfall with the hypnotist. He nodded and held me closer. The waterfall was a sign that I had healed from that death in my previous life. Are you still with me....?

When I think back on that particular past life, my death as a result of sleeping with my father, I had little choice in the matter. I wonder if perhaps that life helped me in this one. We know my father lusted for me starting at a very early age in my current life. Maybe my past life somehow intuitively warned me to reject letting my father touch me in my current life where I had a choice. You can think what you want, but I know and feel, I brought that knowledge with me to this life.

I am now 65 and my father has been dead for 15 years. The mystery of my paralyzed arm when I was five sitting on his lap is still with me. If I could go to past lives under hypnosis, why couldn't I just go back to five years old?

I called my therapist and made an appointment. When I arrived I discussed my thoughts about going back to a specific time in my life. I told him what had happened and how old I was so he knew how far back to take me. I lay down on the couch very apprehensive took a deep breath and under I went! He talked me down in time until I saw my 6 year old brother, Donnie, playing with pennies under the dining room table. He loved to play war with the pennies. I was under the table watching him play when I suddenly heard my father's voice calling to come sit on his lap. I rushed over to him. He lifted me up and I straddled him one leg to the right, the other to the left. Under hypnosis, I am carefully watching myself as I sit on his lap. I try desperately to see his face. I can't see it, I'm afraid. I am only able to envision a blank, gray TV screen. The expression on his face is still escaping me. My therapist brings me out of my hypnosis. He feels that we are close to seeing my father's face but doesn't want to rush me. I was very determined to set my mind free by accomplishing my goal of seeing my father's face. I set an appointment for next week.

When I showed up this time, my therapist told me he was going to help me out by sending grown-up Lanie with little Lanie so I wouldn't be alone. This time I would be watching my little self, but I would also be there as an adult to protect my five-year-old self. I was apprehensive, but I told him I would make my best effort. My determination was stronger than ever, I yearned for full closure on this lifelong episode. What caused the paralysis of my arm? What did I do?

Down the rabbit hole I went finding myself once again in my Detroit home. My brother playing pennies under the dining room table, I had been here before, the big question was could I *finally* see my father's face? He asks me to sit on his lap. I am so happy that he wants to spend time with me. I am straddling him and we tickle each other giggling for a few moments. Slowly his big hand comes up to take my little hand and pushes my hand against the front of his pants. I feel something hard. Both our hands are rubbing his pants. I look up into his face, with tears welling in my eyes, I cried out, "I can see his face! I can see his face!" Tears start flowing down my face. I shout two grown-up Lanie. "I can see his face!"

My father's eyes reveal a lecherous man with a salacious smile of pleasure! I throb with guilt, as if I'm doing something really bad! My arm with the hand on his pants tingles — goes numb! Big Lanie takes me away, holds me asks me if I am okay. She looks into my eyes and tells me you are doing nothing bad. You did nothing wrong.

"Your father is taking advantage of you because you are a little girl, just a child!" Big Lanie brings her face close to my little face bathed in tears, takes both her hands, then holds my face and gently says, "You can let it go now, Lanie. You are okay now. The blame falls to your father. It was no fault of yours. You should feel no guilt!"

I am coming out of hypnosis. I am crying, not a frantic, sobbing cry, but a joyful yet sad realization of relief. Relief! — Finally, I could see his face. How could he do that to me? I was just a little girl. I was his daughter! How could he do that to his own daughter? I began thinking about my therapy session with Dr. Ryan. I told him my arm was paralyzed and he said I was probably traumatized. He said I could possibly have conversion disorder. So I was traumatized by my father actions. And because I was traumatized, I paralyzed my own arm. Talk about a magic trick. I was only five years old. Amazing that at 5 years old, I was so traumatized I could paralyze my arm, and for months!

So how does that make me feel, now that the mystery is over?

Sometimes I feel numb. I don't want to relive the pain he caused me. I get very angry and confused. Mainly, I am disappointed and angry that I didn't have a father in my life. I feel lucky that it wasn't worse. The realization that at 5 years old I could paralyze my arm is absolutely mind boggling! I can't help but wonder what other children have done to themselves when they were molested. It's in the past. I had moved on a long time ago. I think I was one of the lucky ones. I had some inner strength when I was young, that saved me.

I realize my experienced may not be as traumatic as others, but this is *my* story. I believe there are other children out there who are haunted by their fathers or other family members. I am not giving medical nor psychiatric advice. I am just telling my story, and my story refuses to allow anyone to dictate who I am or what my worth is! I will continue to find ways to understand who I am and why I feel the way I do. Right now with Joe I am the happiest I have ever been. I have found peace and I really like myself. I am the silliest person I know and I love that about me. It keeps me happy. Most importantly, I will not use what my father did to me as an *excuse* to not live my life to the fullest!

My Favorite Spiritual Books

Conversations with God: Walsh, Neale Donald
Destiny of Souls: Newton, Michael
Memories of the Afterlife: Newton, Michael
Messages from the Masters: Weiss, Brian
The Prophet: Gibran, Kahliel
The Road Less Traveled: Peck, Scott M.
Testimony of Light: Greaves, Helen
Touched by Angels: Freeman, Eileen Elias

CHAPTER 22
This Might Help — Give It a Shot

Even though I saw my father's face, and understood my trauma, from time to time, the thought of him, would surface in a nagging way. I had a successful experience ridding that annoyance from a new psychic my friend introduced me to, in the form of a — I'm going to call it — a "trick." I would like to share that with you now.

My childhood friend, Barbara, suggested I call a psychic friend of hers for a phone reading. The psychic lives in Philadelphia and I was in California. Kat was her name. Kat had been very helpful reading for Barbara after her husband passed away a year ago. Barbara knows I love psychic readings. We both are eager to learn more about ourselves.

I eagerly dialed Kat's number wondering just how good she was going to be. She answers and asks me right away with what would I like to talk about? I was unprepared for this. I had nothing in mind to talk about. My usually readings start with what the psychic sees in my future. If I am lucky at the session, I can call some passed family member to speak with me. Then they ask if I have any questions.

After a few minutes, I arrive at telling Kat about my father. I had resolved the basic issue of seeing his face, understanding what caused my trauma and paralyzed arm. But nevertheless, my father still popped into my head every now and then which annoyed me. I was tired of wasting energy dealing with him.

She tells me she wants to hear the whole story. She believes she can rid me of these nagging recurring interruptions from my father. I recounted the whole story. Once I had finished my story, she said she needed a little more time and please stay on the line. You can imagine I was wondering what she would be doing while I waited. When you are in the psychic's office or home, you are able to see how they commune with the universe. Psychics may burn incense then speak to their spirit guide or sit quietly to channel someone in the afterlife. But there I was having no idea what she was doing.

About 5 minutes later she got back on the line. She gave me some instructions. "Now, Lanie, this is what we're going to do. I have written your story on several pieces of paper. And now we are going to burn your story and flush the ashes down the toilet."

"We're going to do what?" I said.

Kat must have been writing my story down as I was relaying it to her. I was amazed and bewildered. And now we were about to burn it! This was a first for me. I wasn't quite sure how to feel about this.

She continued, "I have a container in front of me for a small fire in which we are now going to burn your story." I hear Kat light a match and wait for her words. There is a silence while my story is burning.

"Your words and story are now in flames soon to be a pile of ashes. We are now going to send them to oblivion. I want you to visualize your taking my hand as we hold the ashes over the toilet bowl. Watch us as we will now flush these ashes — your story — completely out of your life! Are you ready?

"Yes, I'm ready!"

"Now this is the last time you will ever hear from or think about your father. He will no longer linger in your mind. I will say a few words over these ashes then we will both throw the ashes and flush your father away."

I heard her quietly say something. I couldn't make out the words, but I had a feeling she was talking to the universe about me and my story. She spoke to me again....

"This is it! Watch us as we throw the ashes into the bowl and flush them down." I hear the toilet flush and feel my face flush as well in some kind of new relief.

"From now on you will be entirely free of any thoughts about your father. He will no longer intrude into your mind. You will never want to think about him again nor talk about him again for any reason. Your father will no longer have any effect on you whatsoever!"

I am still shaking my head over this one! The moment I heard the flush of the toilet, I felt my father leave me — gone! I felt somehow lighter, sat up straighter, took a big breath in, let it out, and felt myself in a different space. The space around me seemed free and empty of his invisible presence! I had no idea I was going to talk about my father, but apparently I had just enough unresolved feelings that I needed to be rid of. Unknowingly he still had power over me. I couldn't thank her enough!

I shared my session with Barbara. She was thrilled for me. The whole episode was so rewarding and unexpected!

I am sharing this next and last of my stories with you because later I had occasion to play psychic for myself. Completely without warning I had been on the receiving end of a major coup where I worked. Yes, that's right I was ousted from my position at work! They wanted me to stay and continue to work but not in the same capacity. Thanks, but no thanks. I was really stunned and extremely hurt. I had never been treated that way and it brought me to tears.

I shared what happened to me with my friend, Jan. I also told her all about Kat, my new psychic. So there we were on my porch one afternoon, and Jan with her cute little smile said, "Lanie, why don't you try Kat's toilet trick on that "coup" yourself?" With my mouth open wide, I gasp, "Yes!"

It was midnight that same day. I got out of bed quietly not wanting to wake Joe. I walked to the living room to write out my whole story. I named names and did not hold back on any of the details. Gathering my pages together, I used my kitchen sink as a receptacle for my small fire and started burning my papers. Bad idea! As the flames rose, I realized I needed to throw the ashes down the toilet. Two problems — water in the sink started to dissolve my ashes — I was right under a smoke alarm! My husband was still asleep. I grabbed the burning papers and started blowing the smoke from the papers toward the open window above the sink, hoping the smoke would not set off the alarm. In my rush to the window, the ashes and some of the burning papers kind of went flying. I now had ashes and burning paper on the window ledge, my sink, on my kitchen counter and on my hands. How was I going to get this mess down the toilet? *Down the toilet?*

Down the toilet! These words jabbed my funny bone. What am I doing? I burst out laughing! I covered my mouth quickly as I did not want to wake Joe. I got a mouthful of ashes! The taste of ashes brought me to hysteria! I was having trouble keeping my wits about me! Finally, sweeping as much ashes on a piece of paper as I could find, I made my way to the bathroom. I stood over the toilet bowl, still chuckling.

Standing at the edge of my toilet bowl with my story in hand, I realized the situation was no longer funny. As I stared into the bowl, the water somehow became deeper and darker. I began to feel some kind of communication with a strength the universe was offering me. Looking down into the dark water was like looking into a black whole from the universe. I remembered Kat had said something to the spirit world before she threw the ashes into the toilet. I decided to add my own words and thoughts as well before I flushed my story down the toilet. After saying a few words, I brushed off whatever ashes I had on the paper, flushed the toilet watching the entire mess swirl out of sight. Most of it went down. But I was taking no chances! I was going to make sure this job was done properly. I flushed a second time. Gone! And gone were my sleepless nights.

I am passing this *Kat trick* on to you my readers it might work for you, good luck!

CHAPTER 23
Thinking of Writing Your Memoir?

My 1965 New York City roommate and now close friend, Bonnie Michael, mentioned in one of our phone conversations that she was writing a memoir to leave for her family and friends. I mentioned to her how cool that was and that I certainly couldn't do something like that. Bonnie said immediately, of course you can. I still can hear her voice saying that. But I told her I can't even spell! We laughed! Oh, Lanie, yes you can. Use Siri on your phone! I laughed again and we left it at that. I did not think of it again. Later that day I realized she was the match that struck a flame in me. I turn to my brother, Jimmy, who is a published author with a background in English literature. I asked him if he had the time and the inclination to help me write my memoir. Frankly I didn't even know what I would say or even if I had a story. Jimmy is seven years older than I am, lives in Colorado and we are very close. He has told me that I am one of his heroes. He says this because, as you have already read, my life had its share of ups and downs — thus the title, <u>Haunted yet Undaunted</u>! He said it sounded like a spectacular idea! Thanks to Bonnie and her unquestioningly confidence in me, I am writing my memoir with my brother

Jimmy, my personal wordsmith. Thank you so very much my dear girl friend from 73rd street!

We began writing my memoir, my legacy for my family and friends. This simple goal, recounting my life from five years old to present, evolved into a discovery of who I had truly been. No matter your age, think back when you were five maybe 10 years old. Here you are now. If you are honest, you will realize you had no idea who you were or what you were doing during those years. When you reach my age, you discover how much depended on who you are inside and what kind of luck you would bring to yourself. I continued to wonder about my self-worth for years after my father had made me feel worthless. As I continued to write, I began to get such a positive picture of myself through the years. I was undaunted. I met challenges and resolved them in creative, exciting, and profitable ways. I feel in writing my memoir, I discovered who I really am. And have now grown to believe in and understand *my* true worth. That's what whispering in my ear now.

Now it's time for me to share what you do the *minute* you have completed your memoir. No! You don't go out to dinner and drink a bottle of Champaign!

You visit your local psychic. That exactly what you do! I'm lucky to have my own personal psychic, Glenda, who lives here in Hemet.

I made an appointment to have a reading with her, just before the summer. I mentioned I was going to write my memoir. Glenda said, I would finish the book by December, and that it would be helpful to people and successful.

I did finish by December and now we will just wait and see what happens after publication. It's fun to know what a psychic may find in your future. Glenda always has been right on! She has become someone I can talk with and visit from time to time. Glenda is a very lovely and genuine person.

So we will just wait and see what the universe has in store for me, and possible for you. Give it a try!

You may not have a brother, who is an English Major, you may not have thought of your life as anything to write about, but I challenge you to go back into your life thinking about *your* story. Everyone has a story. This may be your time to discover who you are, and how you got there.

I have written and published my memoir. I am standing at the railing on my front porch in Hemet, California. I am holding my book. I'm looking into the dusk over the mountains. Jimmy had told me that one day I would be holding my book in my hand as if it were a miracle! I stop to open the book and check out some of the writing. Remembering how Jimmy and I put it together with Joe by my side. All the fun, all the laughs, all the corrections!

I looked up into the universe feeling its energy fill me with joy. I did it! I made it and I didn't have to turn into a *boy*! I asked the universe if this was all there was for me? At 77 should I rest now? Is there nothing new in store for me after having written my memoir? The universe answered, NO! I looked out just beyond the mountains. I am certain that right now as I stand here, I feel some new challenge, project, discovery just peeking out over my horizon. Rest! Who needs rest, when there is so much out there calling me? I bet if you listen hard enough, you will hear something calling *you*.

My name is Leonie "Lanie" Norton. I am the girl next door who graduated from Glen Rock high school in New Jersey.

I am no longer haunted.

I remain undaunted!

Leonie "Lanie" Norton
and Jim Norton

To quote Winston Churchill:

"Now this is not the end. It is not even the beginning
of the end. But it is, perhaps, the end of the beginning."

"See you next time".

CHAPTER 24
Thank You Joe

Throughout our 16 years together, Joe has supported me in every venture I have undertaken — no questions asked! Always with a loving, understanding smile! He has always been my go-to guy with a shoulder to lean on.

I was not surprised that as I began writing my memoir, Joe said he wanted to help. He designed the book cover, organized all the written files in the computer, composed my photo collages and researched when necessary. And most importantly, he talked me through a few melt down during the course of my writing.

Thank you, Joe, for giving me so much of your time. I want you to know I couldn't have written my book without you, and that's why, "I pay you the big bucks!" (He always laughs when I say that!) Having a husband say he is proud of you means everything to me.

Chapter 25

My Brother Jimmy

Jimmy, Jimmy, Bo Binny, Fe Fi Fo Finny, Jimmy! That's my fun loving big brother Jimmy — my co writer and wordsmith. We have talked almost once a day since our mom passed, 30 years ago. Even with a 7 year age difference we are very close. He has lived through my 3 husbands and that was no easy task. When his wife, Ida May, who was his soul mate, passed eight years ago, we kept in close touch because he needed support during his grief. This close support we had for each other educated both of us about each other's emotional entities.

Jimmy taught public secondary school English for 20 years and is a published author. This intimate knowledge of each other, my story, and his language skills allowed us to collaborate on my memoir.

He has produced an authentic life story complete with my true emotional responses. He has done an amazing job putting those emotions into words. I especially want to thank him for that. I feel as if he were right there with me the whole time.

The beautiful part of writing this together is that we have become even closer (if that's possible). Writing together was so much fun, a once-in-a-lifetime experience — I will never forget!

I feel that this is so much *our* book — since we both lived my good times, scary times, and sad times together as we collaborated. After completing the book we both feel we have grown as people and writers.

Thank you for writing my memoir with me — you have done one hell of a job! I will always be so very grateful. Writing this book with you and

my husband Joe, has given me a greater sense of bride and self-worth, —
that I never would have imagined. What a joy for me at age 77.

I will always treasure this amazing, beautiful, time.

lanenorton@dcemail.com